THEY ALL HAD EYES:

Confessions of a Vivisectionist

MICHAEL A. SLUSHER

Illustrations by Ninette Guerrero Selva

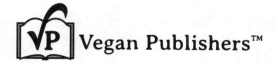

Vegan Publishers™

Published by:
Vegan Publishers
Danvers, MA
www.veganpublishers.com

Illustrations by Ninette Guerrero Selva
Cover and text design by Nicola May Design

Printed in the United States of America

ISBN: 9781940184234

THANK YOU

To my father for handing down to me his passion for all the sciences.
To my mother for providing a lifetime of unconditional love and support.
To my sister who learned from my many mistakes.
To my wife who constantly helps me from making more of them.

ACKNOWLEDGEMENTS

This book is dedicated to the many animals whom I tortured and killed in the name of science. If there is a hell, I will spend it forever looking into their eyes.

I sincerely thank my wife for her love, unwavering support, and encouragement, even though I was revealing and reliving the most disturbing aspects of my past.

Thanks to Casey at Vegan Publishers for having faith in my writing abilities when I didn't and his insistence that this story needed to be told. Thanks also to the many contributors to the Indiegogo campaign, a crowd-funding effort that was essential in getting this book launched. I could not have done it without you. Special mention and a very special thanks go to Ashley Cantwell, Beth Chappelle, Dr. Gloria Feltham (BVSc, MRCVS, BSc, Animal Behavior and Welfare), Patricia Ellen Knudsen, Dacia Thorson, and especially Kathleen Hampton, for their extremely generous contributions.

I would be remiss if I didn't thank the wonderful and talented graphic artist Ninette Guerrero Selva for her fantastic work on this book. Her cover art perfectly captured a key moment in my career and her chapter drawings tactfully convey images of things that should never be seen. Her humble refusal to accept payment was, of course, ignored.

I wish to thank my online friends for putting up with all my whining and complaining and for both their snarky sarcasm and support—you are my true friends, even though we may have never met in person (yet).

Finally, thanks to the cats who run my home for allowing me to pet them while I told them how very sorry I am for my past sins against fellow Earthlings. If drooling on me is a sign of their forgiveness, then I am truly blessed.

CONTENTS

FOREWORD

I love science. Like Michael Slusher, I grew up with a fascination for biology and animals. I also had a natural inclination to nurture others. So, I decided as a kid that one day I was going to become a doctor. Naturally, I thought that my desire to heal and my awe of living things would fit together nicely. Right?

I got a rude awakening during my high school biology class. One day, my teacher handed each pair of students a live frog to study. Our class that day was a riot as we all played with the frogs (under the guise of learning their biology) and scrambling after them as they jumped around the classroom in chaos. The frogs were adorable and my fellow classmates and I were delighted in them.

The next day, we arrived in class to find all our frogs dead and laid out on our tables, ready for us to dissect them. The contrast between the symphony of a classroom of frogs chirping and thumping around the day before and the still silence that awaited us that day was absolutely jarring to me. When I asked my teacher why did the frogs have to be killed, he responded as though the answer was obvious and sufficient: "it's part of the curriculum of the class."

I was suddenly confronted with a harsh reality about the world of science and medicine: living beings—animals-- are nothing more than tools. This was a reality I faced frequently on my path to becoming a neurologist.

My biology teacher was just one in a long line of individuals I encountered who never questioned their use of animals as mere tools. I worked with fellow neurologists who crushed the spines of cats in labs, but cherished their dogs at home; and technicians who harmed animals in research labs on weekdays, but rescued animals on weekends. I often found myself asking how do otherwise thoughtful people fall into the business of harming animals? Their answer to my question was always the same: we have to in the name of science and human health. But is it really true that we have to hurt animals to heal ourselves or did we just get trapped into this way of thinking?

Finally, with this book, we get some answers. Slusher, who grew up with a love of animals, shows us how easily anyone can get trapped into a way of thinking without questioning his or her actions. He takes us inside the world of animal laboratories—a world that most readers will never otherwise see. Slusher shows us, better than any other author I have read, what lives are like for animals in laboratories. With exquisite detail, we not only see the lives of these animals with our minds, but we can hear, smell, and even taste the world they are forced to live, suffer, and die in.

Although Slusher's experience inside animal labs took place several years ago, the unfortunate reality is that little has changed for the animals in the ensuing decades. Our laws and regulations are pitiful and the well-being of animals almost always takes a back seat to other interests. In the name of research, anything can be, and arguably has been, done to animals, no matter how much suffering it causes. Hundreds of millions of animals are poisoned, burned, dismembered, blinded, infected, crushed, and electrocuted every year. And to add insult to injury, much of it is paid for by our tax dollars.

Although reading the descriptions of what is done to animals can be hard for many to stomach, this book is so important because it helps us to understand how individuals can rationalize these experiments and dissociate themselves from the suffering they cause animals. Throughout the book, we get glimpses of Slusher's doubts or qualms about his actions—especially with certain animals he interacted with or procedures he was asked to conduct on them. And we see how Slusher and others, often through dark humor (like referring to the mouse gas chambers as "mauschwitz"), repressed those doubts.

Slusher shows us how cruelty becomes normalized. It's a vital lesson for humanity. By understanding how cruelty becomes business as usual, we can perhaps learn how to free people from this mindset. And it's an urgent lesson because we are learning that not only are animal experiments bad for animals, they're also bad for us. For decades, researchers experimented on animals with blinders on—rarely questioning not only the ethics, but also the scientific rationale behind these horrendous experiments.

Fortunately that's changing. More scientists are taking a hard look at the data on animal experiments to determine how relevant they are for human diseases and for improving our lives. What the evidence is overwhelmingly showing is that animal experiments are outdated and are extremely poor at predicting what we will find in humans.

In the past, experimenters have said that animals were helpful in understanding human physiology and anatomy at a very basic level. Today we are well beyond that, instead delving into the subtle nuances of molecular biology. The way medicine is practiced today, animal experiments are simply too unreliable for telling us what will happen in humans. Despite the similarities we share with other animals in our physiology, it's the differences between species that cause problems. These differences make animals poor substitutes to understanding human physiology and curing human diseases.

More than nine out of ten drugs that are found safe and effective in animals are later found to be unsafe or ineffective in humans. Thousands of people fall sick each year in the U.S. from new drugs because animal experiments mislead us into believing these drugs are safe. Perhaps even more troubling, we may have tossed out medical treatments and even cures that didn't work in animals, but would have worked wonderfully in humans. Animal experimentation is not only hurting animals, but also ourselves.

There are other ways—better ways—to study human biology. We can find more effective cures and drugs by directing our resources into discovering and using more accurate human-based testing methods. Testing methods like human organs-on-a-chip, cognitive computing technologies, 3D printing of human living tissues, and the Human Toxome Project are far superior to animal experiments because they are based on *human* biology.

The good news is that we can better heal humans without hurting animals. We are not trapped into doing animal experiments. If someone like Slusher, who spent many years experimenting on animals, can find a way out, then there is hope that one day the miserable business of animal experimentation will end.

— Aysha Akhtar, MD, MPH, neurologist, public health specialist, and author of *Animals and Public Health: Why Treating Animals Better is Critical to Human Welfare*

PREFACE

I am a monster.

My family and friends disagree with that assessment, but it was hard not to think of myself that way as I contemplated the book that I had to write. And it *needed* to be written.

My experiences as a biomedical research associate were painful to write about and will undoubtedly be rather painful to read. The source of my pain was partially the shame and embarrassment for having been so blind to my own actions, but more deeply, it originated from my empathy for the victims. It's nearly impossible to conceive what they thought or felt. The excruciating nature of their experiences was far more profound than any gruesomeness ever expressed in any horror novel. As soon as I'd try to imagine what they must have felt, my brain wanted to shut down. However, I know that the suffering I felt writing this was minuscule in comparison to what they experienced.

I didn't enter into this project lightly or casually. Nobody likes to recognize the major failings in their lives. We also don't want to be proven wrong when we perceive ourselves as loving, compassionate beings while our work history seems to say otherwise. Therefore, the very idea of confronting my past and then exposing my crimes of morality for the world to see was an almost inconceivable and truly terrifying concept. I was deeply afraid that I would lose many friends. Was I going to be ostracized by the animal rights community, forever forced out from the groups of animal-lovers that I now considered myself to be part of? Would people who still consider animal research to be a necessary evil also shun me as an irresponsible whistle-blower with little scientific or even rational credibility? Despite these misgivings, I knew this book had to be written. People had to know the truth, regardless of any social repercussions or damage to my reputation.

For many years, I didn't examine this part of my past with any real scrutiny. It simply had been my job, and since I was no longer working in that field, I didn't need to revisit it. Until five years ago, I was like everybody else. I ate meat, eggs, and dairy. I wore wool, silk, and leather. I used toiletries that were tested on animals. I went to zoos and aquariums. I didn't really think about how my actions and money exploited animals. Of course, I also called myself an "animal lover" and had long ago given up veal and SeaWorld because of the cruelty, but I was still happily wearing blinders in every other facet of my life. While most of us ate meat since early childhood and some people are hunters or fishing enthusiasts, very few of us have ever actually been egg or dairy workers, slaughterhouse employees, or vivisectionists. I therefore had very few friends to rely on who would understand my particular situation as I began to take off my blinders. The more I dug up old memories, the more I realized that I would have to go there alone. And I dug deep.

It wasn't long before the nightmares began.

I was walking alone through a dark hallway with dim, flickering lights when I looked down and saw hundreds of mice and rats all running past me down the corridor and turning into an even darker hallway. I followed them, but they always stayed ahead of me, turning corners and following corridors without an obvious destination but with a singleness of mind. I didn't know what they were headed towards or why, but I felt compelled to follow, faster and faster, until I was running to keep up. From all sides, more and more of the small white rodents joined the wide, living stream, covering every inch of floor in their accelerating dash. I tried to call out and get their attention, but they ignored me. Not one of them gave even a single glance in my direction. There seemed to be a lot of yelling in my ears, but I didn't know from whom or what or why. They were just incomprehensible voices that grew louder and louder. The river of rodents eventually turned a blind corner and I felt sure that I had finally caught up, but when I rounded the corner, I saw nothing but a big gray steel door. I swung it open as my heart beat against my ribs. I knew it wasn't going to be pleasant, but the sight of what lay behind that door made me gasp. Thousands of tiny pink lights were glowing brightly in a huge black space. At first, I didn't know what they were, but as more and more of the little glowing pinpoints of light began to illuminate the sinister cavern, I could see that they were eyes—the pink eyes of the thousands of rats and mice I was trying so desperately to follow. They sat in silence as more and more of them turned to face me. I thought about screaming, but worried it would make them charge at me, so I just stood there, afraid to move. Then, slowly, their eyes started going dark. One by one, they blinked closed, ending the light in each pink orb, never to shine again. They were going to be all gone, and soon I would be alone in the dark. I finally screamed out in a panic, "STOP! Please don't go! I'm sorry!" but it was too late. As the last of the little pink lights went out, I awoke alone in my bed, soaked in sweat.

I had no idea that such dreams were going to remain with me. Often, they were simply gruesome: I saw a rabbit who seemed so happy and serene, resting on a table. When I approached to pet him, he rolled onto his side, and his entrails poured out onto the tabletop. Occasionally, they were simply sad memories of lost cats and other pets who had died from old age or disease (or worse). Other dreams were about angry monkeys who terrified me, or about playful dogs who didn't seem to care who I was, even though I held a horrible secret. But no matter whom it was that I faced in my dreams, they always looked at me . . . and I couldn't tear myself from their eyes. They all had eyes.

I could no longer look at the hamsters, rats, birds, and other small animals when I bought cat litter and dog food at the local pet store. They all reminded me of what I did and what I was. Each little furry life, now an inexpensive commodity in a cage, was a disposable prisoner to later be tormented or ignored (or both) by some child. I felt horror and anger at the fate they were destined to, and then I had to remind myself that I was guilty of doing many worse things to them—I had no right to be so indignant.

And yet. . . .

Just because I had once performed actions that I was not proud of didn't mean that I had to turn a blind eye towards the fate of other animals currently in the path of destruction. I realized that simply reconciling my past in my own mind was not enough. I had to change the future as well. Nearly fifty years old, I began to ruminate upon what it meant to be a vivisectionist-turned-vegan. I realized that the best thing I could possibly do at this point in my life would be to share my history with others. I needed to let it be known that such horrific activities are not only occurring on college campuses and in nearly all pharmaceutical and cosmetics companies, but that they are extremely commonplace in those institutions and entirely blessed by the Powers That Be. And not just blessed, but *required*.

Some specific details, including names and places, have been altered or omitted for legal reasons. Because I have pushed most of these events down deep into the recesses of my mind over the years and dragging them out again for this book has been something of an ordeal, there were bound to be errors of both omission and fact. However, I have done my best to recollect and record everything as fully and accurately as possible. The reader should be cautioned: I did not withhold any of the horrors.

It is for the laboratory animals that this was written, not only to expose some of the practices routinely performed *In The Name Of Science*, but also to help ensure that their lives were not sacrificed totally in vain. I don't ask for your forgiveness, but I do ask for your action to bring an end to this and other institutionalized acts of barbarism against our fellow Earthlings.

CHAPTER ONE

A Zoologist from Birth

The brain was particularly tough to extract. Never having taken a brain out of a skull before, I discovered that it involved a lot of blood and cracking of bone. It never occurred to me to skin the rat first, and thus there was hair sticking to the blood on my fingers. Finally, after much frustration, that fragile lump of gray cranial fat was free with only a few chunks missing. When we were finally all done with this project, we had a clear plastic cube containing a liver and another one with a heart, one with a kidney, and one with a lung. The brain cube was supposed to be the most interesting, but the uncured plastic was still slightly tacky to the touch, leaving my cloudy fingerprints on the surface. There were also many bubbles within the cubes, impeding the view of the disemboweled rat's organs. As a thirteen year old, my skills at properly curing plastic were somewhat lacking. I don't remember what grade my girlfriend received in exchange for the rat's life.

———□——————————————————————□———

I was raised in a family of educators. My mother taught special education and my two sisters would also become teachers. My father was a teacher and scientist too, but could best be described as a true Renaissance man and a certified, card-carrying Mensa genius, able to play multiple instruments and speak several languages (including Chinese and Russian). He was an avid collector of many things, from old Navajo pottery and rare sixteenth-century books to obscure scientific instruments and countless chemicals.

We moved a lot. My father also collected various college degrees and changed jobs frequently, but wherever we moved, he always brought along his laboratory. For example, as a child I lived in a small town in central Illinois. I didn't know that my family was much different than my friends' families, but I also didn't know anyone else who had a home quite like ours. The upstairs was unremarkable and similar to every other middle class home in the 1970s. We had the obligatory avocado-green kitchen appliances, thick shag carpeting, and old rotary-dial telephones. The finished basement, however, was another story.

Descending the wooden stairs, your nose would always be greeted with an acrid chemistry-set smell that I could never fully explain to my friends. Upon turning on the lights, you were faced with old, rickety shelves full of musty books lining an entire wall. Tables and counters were covered with electronic equipment that only my father knew the function of. Countless rows of drawers were stuffed with every manner of crazy tool, gadget, and spare part suitable only for the evil laboratories seen on *Midnight Monster Chiller Horror Theater*, which I stayed up to watch in the dark each week religiously. Another set of shelves was stuffed precariously with bottles and jars containing wondrous and mysterious compounds, each one more hazardous and lethal than the last. Skull-and-crossbones adorned more than a few labels, and a couple had "DANGER!" handwritten in large red letters, impossible to miss.

Strangely, there were delicious treasures on those shelves too. A small vial of pure peppermint crystals contained something magical in its intensity and beauty, as even the smallest white shard of this spiky substance would overwhelm your mouth and nose. I never knew my young sinuses could ever feel so clear, when my father allowed me to sample this rare treat. A small brown bottle, with a cracked black cap and a label with lettering long-since faded, yielded a glass wand within dripping a thick amber syrup. Touching the wand to my tongue and letting just a single drop coat my mouth convinced me that not all the chemicals were scary—this one was as sweet as honey. That's pure glycerin, he told me matter-of-fact, with only a hint of an alchemist's flair. He often told me of his fondness for Vincent Price, and in my young mind, I always associated them together, the mischievous mad scientist and my dad—interchangeable.

He sternly and repeatedly told me not to eat any more of those two substances, for they would make me sick, and to never *ever* eat anything else in his basement lab. I didn't know whether he was lying or not, and in hindsight, he probably just didn't want me to eat up all his mint and glycerin. Nevertheless, I took his words to heart. I saw what some of the other chemicals he collected had done to the insects and rodents that he considered to be pests. I wasn't going to let my curiosity get the upper hand.

One glass jar was particularly creepy. It had a thick layer of cotton on the bottom with a perforated floor resting above the cotton. The tight-fitting lid contained the certain death within, as the jar had both a skull and a red "CAUTION!" label on it. This is where many interesting and almost alien creatures were placed. Not only your average beetles or spiders, but also the most amazing and rare bugs one could ever imagine found their way here, anytime my father found them. I often watched a hapless arthropod writhe in its articulated agony as it slowly died in this gas chamber made specifically for that purpose. Later, my dad would stab pins through their bodies and mount them inside wooden cigar boxes, for display and hoarding. This was considered normal behavior for those with an interest in entomology. And it was Science.

My father had no shortage of interests and always shared his knowledge about each of them with me, especially science. Biology was always my favorite, however, especially when it dealt with animals—zoology. Botany was boring; chemistry was confusing; math was impossible. But if it involved zoology, well, then you were talking my language! My favorite aspect of my dad's collections (much more interesting to me than the stamp and coin collections he was so proud of) was all the animal specimens. In addition to all the insects in boxes, he had countless seashells, skulls, pelts, and fossils. They provided me with hours of interest, and I studied every aspect of each one as if it were the only specimen of that species left on Earth.

In line with my dad's own interest in zoology, for as long as I remember, he also had pet snakes. He wasn't one of those herpetology hoarders with hundreds of the cold-blooded animals stacked and displayed in tanks, tubs, and cages all over the house, but he always had at least one or two docile pet snakes that he liked to bring out and play with. It was a natural part of my childhood.

In order to feed the snakes, of course, he had to provide small animals and he therefore always had a colony of mice that he bred. I remember marveling at the process of pregnancy—the roundness of the female and the births of so many babies at once—and feeling fortunate to having witnessed several births as they happened. The babies would be weaned and eating solid food in just a few weeks, and she would be ready to breed again even before that. His small snakes (and pet tarantulas) would be given those newborn "pinkies," the almost universal name for hairless and blind baby mice just a few days old. If there were more than he needed, he would simply freeze them alive. He explained to me that it was painless, as they would simply fall asleep. I was skeptical, but why would I question this man who seemingly knew everything. There were always frozen baby mice in baggies in the freezer, but his larger snakes received adult mice. Ideally, they were served alive, as the snake preferred to eat them warm, but sometimes freezer-stored adults were also simply thawed out and served dead.

As gruesome as it seems now, as a child I was fascinated by the sudden and violent way in which these carnivores naturally caught, killed, and ate their prey. I saw it as the "circle of life" and knew that the snakes and spiders were only doing what they had evolved to do: survive. There was no immorality or abuse to it; my dad tossing a mouse into the snake's terrarium and my interest in watching it kill and eat were simply a real-life version of beloved episodes of *Wild Kingdom* or *National Geographic* on television. My dad was raised on a farm and, like him, I too felt that some animals were simply meant to be used as food for other animals (including us).

One of his favorite snakes that he kept for many years was a boa constrictor. When she outgrew the adult mouse stage, my dad started breeding and feeding her rats. Extra baby rats would go to other smaller snakes, or join the frozen mice in our freezer, much to my mom's continual protestations. Eventually, the snake outgrew rats, so my dad started ordering hatchling chickens, whom he would raise to a size suitable for the snake and then freeze them as well. Needless to say, my mom was not at all happy about this either. She refused to watch the snakes eat and considered the whole hobby gross. I sided with my dad on the vital importance of feeding these scaly pets; I too had my own pet snakes by this point. Eventually, the boa outgrew our home and our ability to safely care for her, and she was given to a local zoo. I think my mom was afraid that she would escape and eat one of our dogs (or my sister).

While the activities involved in this hobby seem horrible, it's really not at all unusual for amateur herpetologists, people who study reptiles and amphibians. There is an entire sub-culture of herpetology buffs who legally collect and breed exotic reptiles and amphibians. The more rare and exotic the creature, the better. However, this demand has also created a huge illegal trade in these poor animals, many (or most) of whom die as a result of attempted smuggling. Sadly, while the illegal parrot trade is somewhat well known, very little is discussed about the trade of exotic reptiles. No doubt, this silence on the subject reflects the human instinct-influenced tendency to dislike and fear them to begin with.

As a teen and young adult, I too went on to collect snakes, lizards, frogs, and turtles as pets (although I preferred the aquatic nature of turtles and frogs to the others). I too bred or bought small mice (and crickets) to be used as food. I never had enough money for the expensive highly exotic animals, but I certainly contributed to the popularity of the industry. I even became the treasurer of a local herpetology association, a nonprofit group formed by fellow enthusiasts who felt that our mission was to help people understand that "herps make good pets." Our mission was also to teach proper husbandry, bring awareness to illegal smuggling, and help curb the large numbers of unwanted reptiles that are dumped at local animal shelters or released into the wild. I thought I was doing good work for the animals while still enjoying keeping them captive in unnaturally tiny enclosures.

Like most adolescents in the 1970s, long before video games, cable TV, and the Internet, my summers were filled with adventures outdoors. I loved to play in and around the muddy creek behind my suburban house, catching crawdads, fish, snakes, salamanders, turtles, insects, and other poor critters unfortunate enough to be noticed by me. But I didn't just spend my summers mindlessly tormenting small animals. That was just something I did between neighborhood baseball games, G.I. Joes, model rockets, bb guns, Hot Wheels, model trains, and staging elaborate military dioramas on the banks of the creek. From my dad's castoffs and the occasional lucky discovery, I too had built a small collection of animal skulls and bones that I cherished. But overall, I was just your average kid who happened to have a mad scientist for a father.

At the age of thirteen I moved from Illinois to northern New Jersey, and while my focus was often diverted to all the trials and tribulations of being a teenager, my interest in zoology didn't wane. I started collecting more pets—an iguana, a couple of snakes, rats, mice, gerbils, and for a short time, a terrified squirrel I had caught in a live trap. I helped my girlfriend with her science project, which involved dissecting and preserving rat organs in clear plastic. Everything was going fairly normal.

That is, until we moved to Liberia.

Before the country was ravaged by civil war in 1979, the Liberians were in the process of converting their cash crops from the rubber plantations started by Firestone to bananas and other agricultural goods. My father had a graduate degree in plant pathology, and, based on similar work he previously performed in Taiwan, he was hired by the Liberian government to assist as a consultant in this process. This move brought a whole new explosion of life experiences to my teenaged self.

Living in equatorial Africa was clearly a lot different than living in suburban America. I suddenly found my passion for all things animal-related renewed, as each insect, bird, and lizard I encountered was now totally foreign to me. Growing up, I had always seen the many pinned insects and stuffed animals that my father had brought back from Taiwan and marveled at their exotic features and beauty, but this was different. These African animals were not only vastly foreign from what I knew before, but they were vibrant and *alive*. I was excited about this as I enrolled in tenth-grade Biology in the American School: I was going to study West African wildlife!

Instead, our class simply dissected standard-issue formaldehyde-preserved earthworms, frogs, and fish.

Wait, this isn't wildlife research. . . . This is merely what they would have taught me back in New Jersey, I realized.

Since my enthusiasm for Biology was nonetheless clear to the teacher, he made me his laboratory assistant, setting up labs for various classes and (probably more important to him) cleaning them up afterward. In the process, however, I learned about empiricism and how the Scientific Method worked. This was science! I was soon sent out into the bush to collect specimens for his other classes, always being warned to watch out for the aggressive green-and-black mambas, as well as the deadly cassava snake. I brought back giant land snails as big as my fist, colorful frogs, and numerous exotic insects and arachnids, both giant and tiny. After school, I discovered that monkey parts ("bush meat") were sold in the marketplace and I soon brought back heads to clean for their skulls. I even had a pet civet cat, much to my mother's dismay.

I was in heaven.

I was a fairly skinny kid, and approaching six feet tall, I was also taller than most of the other kids in my class. Like many kids in the 1970s, I had long hair—something I had throughout most of my life, unless I was looking for a "real" job and had to clean up my appearance. I was self-conscious about my looks, however, especially by my supposedly large lips, which I used to be teased about in junior high school. Despite my shyness and low self-confidence, I still managed to find a girlfriend—a nice girl from Spain whose parents worked at the Voice of America radio station compound, located outside of town.

In the nine short months we lived there, and mostly without my parent's knowledge, I learned how to fire a shotgun, ride motorcycles, drive cars, and smoke cigarettes (in addition to another plant). I became friends with the Denmark ambassador's son and whenever visiting his home, it was somehow normal that, as a sixteen year old, I would eat caviar, smoke cigars, and drink wine with him and his parents. I often went to discotheques in downtown Monrovia where I drank Bloody Marys with my French art teacher while declining the advances of prostitutes. I was quickly becoming rather European and living a teenager's dream. It was short-lived, however.

One day while surfing with some friends at a popular beach, I learned that the country was erupting into civil war. Each week, I somehow managed to surf away from deadly riptides, jagged rocks, and shark-filled areas of the beach, but I couldn't avoid the collapse of a nation. As the violence grew, my family decided it would be in our best interest to leave as soon as possible. With a curfew in place and bullets literally whizzing overhead, we managed to get on one of the last flights out of the country.

Being back in New Jersey was jarring for me, as I could no longer live the high life as a young adult and had to learn how to be a bored and aimless teenager again in middle class suburban America. To say I floundered at this point is an understatement. For a short time I thought I might become a taxidermist, having caught, killed, and stuffed a squirrel. That wasn't a very positive experience for me, however, and my enthusiasm for education and biology were nearly extinguished while I proceeded to delve deeply into recreational drugs. I struggled to complete high school.

Finally, a couple of years after getting my head back together and after a couple of failed attempts to go to college, I landed a job weighing rats in a small biotech start-up.

It seemed innocent enough.

CHAPTER TWO

Hypox Rats

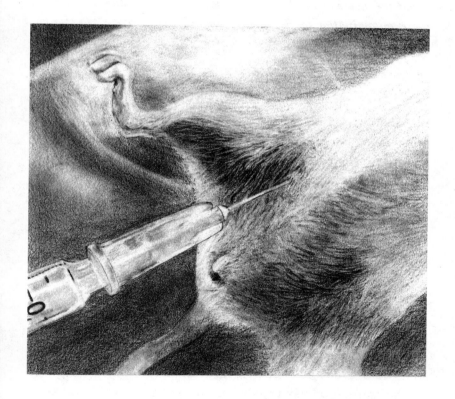

Ironically, it was a "humane" mousetrap they used to control both wild and escaped mice. It consisted of a squared tube of plastic, about two and a half inches across and ten inches long. It had a forty-five-degree bend in the middle and a trap door. The trap was placed on the floor along a wall, with the open entrance against the ground, while the back end with the bait inside angled up off the floor. When a mouse enters, they head towards the back of the trap, causing the whole thing to tilt down and the trap door to close. The reason to use humane traps eluded me, though. I thought that it was odd for the animal facility to care about the plight of a loose or wild mouse when so many of them died at our hands each day. It turned out that I was right — they didn't care about the mouse at all. However, a dead mouse in a kill-trap brought more contamination to the facility than one caught alive. At least, I figured, they received a final meal before they were killed and disposed of.

How exciting! I have a job working with animals, doing real science!

I was twenty-two years old and had been floundering for the past few years since high school. Trying to recover from several disastrous years of substance abuse, my aborted attempts at college only reinforced the fact that I was not mature enough to plan my life, much less succeed. I had recently worked a few minimum wage jobs: security guard, pet shop clerk, indoor corporate landscaping (also known as "watering plants in the shopping mall"). But nothing really got me very interested in life beyond the science fiction novels I was always reading. I was simply existing.

Finally, I found a position at a small biotech start-up that sounded rather fun and paid a little bit more than minimum wage. This was in 1985 and there were many small companies riding high on the prospect of making fabulous money exploring biotechnology (most of these companies would later fail). Applied Lipids was founded on the theory that liposomes, microscopic bubbles of fats, could, for example, be used to transport therapeutic drugs to the sites of disease as a way of increasing their effectiveness. There was also potential for liposomes to reduce the toxicity of many drugs while still maintaining their potency. The company was working on anti-cancer, anti-fungal, and many other therapeutic endeavors.

My job was to weigh rats. I had owned rats as pets before, so I was not squeamish about the task involved and it couldn't have been a simpler job. You pick up a rat (lab rats have long been bred to be thoroughly tame), note the ID number on her ear tag, place her into the metal basket on the scale, and record the weight. Then grab the next rat and do the same thing until you have weighed them all. Simple!

I had no idea what kind of rats these were until after I started. Or what would become of them.

The company was located in a suburban high-tech industrial park, in a single-story building. Inside, there were two main labs, a line of offices on the perimeter, and a suite of animal rooms off one of the labs. The business offices were in another section entirely, as "the suits" preferred to avoid the lab. On my tour, I was taken to one of the rat rooms and shown the cages and work space. The rats in this room were being used in other studies, since the study I was to work on had not yet been started.

The rat room was amazing! Every surface was spotless, from floor to ceiling. It had a slight musky smell, but it was earthy and not at all unpleasant. A lab bench was to the right as I walked in. It was a solid slab of black material, with a deep sink in the middle, and stretched the entire length of the room. Older labs used actual slate for the benches and sinks, but this company, being new, used an epoxy-composite material. Beneath the bench were drawers and cabinets, and yet more cabinets were mounted above the well-lit bench. There was a row of electrical outlets along the full length of the back of the bench; and a red "sharps box" sat at the end, a safe receptacle for depositing used syringes and needles. Everything was so new and clean. Even the floor had rounded corners at its junction with the walls, so no filth could ever accumulate in them. Fluorescent lights in the ceiling ensured adequate illumination, while a timer mounted above the wall switch set the appropriate light/dark cycles. It was very clinical and made me think of a veterinary exam room, but without any decor or posters of dogs, ticks, and heartworms.

On the opposite side of the room from the bench were two large rolling stainless steel shelving units, four shelves high. On each shelf were clear rectangular plastic boxes in neat rows. Metal placards hung from the lips of the boxes, each containing an index card showing the details for that particular box. The same arrangement was repeated on the other side of the shelving unit, so the shelves effectively had a front and a back. The boxes had a stainless steel wire clip-on lid, with a large indented "V" going fully across the center, from left to right. Resting in this "V" was a water bottle, with the sipper tube inserted into the cage, and a generous amount of "Rat Chow." Yes, this is what it's called, because Purina makes it specifically for laboratory rats. The food is comprised of beige, dense nuggets, formed into rounded rectangular shapes about an inch long. It smells similar to a grassy dog biscuit and is about the same texture. The rats chew at the chow with their noses between the wire in order to feed. This highly consistent and controlled diet is all the rats and mice ever get to eat.

I didn't know it at the time, but this room and the cages were almost identical to nearly every other rodent room I was to work in—cold, impersonal, and sterile. Exactly the right setting to help ensure that one's mind also stayed in exactly the same cold and clinical context, leaving all emotion and any traces of empathy at the door.

The rats arrived. I was picturing the full-grown animals that I saw in other cages in the lab and had also owned as pets as a child, but they were nothing like that. While I was told about the study and the fact that the rats I would be weighing were smaller "hypox" rats, I didn't expect what I saw. The animal facility staff had already put them into their cages, but I really didn't think these were the right animals. They were so small, no larger than a gerbil. They were like cute little toy rats, although somewhat fragile and weak looking, and required a warmer room than other rats. Their pink eyes looked at me apprehensively as I tilted a cage towards me to look at them better. They were only five weeks old. They looked scared.

These little white rodents all had surgical staples on the front of their necks. "Hypox," it was explained to me, is short for *hypophysectomy*. This is a procedure where the pituitary gland is removed from the rat's brain at a young age (twenty-five days old), through a hole made in their trachea. This loss of the pituitary gland has many detrimental effects on the animal, but for our purposes, the desired effect was stunted growth. Surgical modification prior to shipping is a common service provided by laboratory animal breeders and hypophysectomized rats are a very common animal model used for research on growth hormones. This was not some strange and unique group of animals; this was business as usual.

Our particular study was meant to establish whether a liposome-encapsulated bovine growth hormone (BST) would be as effective as the non-encapsulated free hormone. The theory was that liposomes could provide a delayed-release mechanism when administering the hormone to cows, thus reducing the frequency of injections.

Each animal required identification for this study, and in rats, ear-tags are often used. A special tool resembling a pair of pliers and a sleeve of numbered metal clips is made specifically for this purpose. Grabbing the little rats around their body, my thumb and index finger circled their shoulders and forced their front arms to cross under their neck. This effectively immobilized them and allowed me to staple the metal clip through their ear. Most of the time, the rats never struggled much, passivity being bred into their nature, but once the ear was pierced, they usually squirmed about in pain and tried to turn and bite, their eyes rolling around trying to locate a means of escape. For this reason, I always wore Kevlar mesh gloves when holding rats in any restraining fashion. Once I tagged them and took an initial weight, they were returned to their original cages, where they quickly ran to the far corner and huddled in fear.

So I was finally weighing rats. As it turned out, the weighing of research animals before, during, and after each study was a task that was nearly always performed, regardless of the species or the study, but this mundane work was still a big deal for me. I felt important! Before the study started, I had to weigh and record each of the rats to make sure the surgeries were fully successful. Any rats that gained more than two grams per week during this preliminary month-long waiting period were rejected from the study. I used a triple-beam balance that was fitted with lidded metal bowl, about the size of large mixing bowl. The bowl had dozens of half-inch holes perforated all around it. A rat went in, I placed the lid on top, and then did my best to figure out the weight of the little creature as she rustled about in her cold, circular pen. As I weighed and removed each rat, the level of urine and feces in the bowl accumulated. Rats, like most animals, will urinate and defecate in response to stress, so I had to rinse out the bowl occasionally so the weights didn't become skewed. With rats this small, those relatively small accumulations of waste made a difference.

Then came the time for injections to begin. My supervisor, a very friendly and unassuming researcher who didn't seem to have a cruel bone in her body, showed me how to give intramuscular injections. I used the same method of restraint as the ear-tagging. Picking them up by their tail, I removed each rat from their cage and placed them on the bench top. While still holding their tail with my left hand to keep them from escaping, my Kevlar-protected right hand firmly grasped them around the chest, again crossing their arms in front of them. I practiced injections of saline on the rejected animals, stabilizing their rear legs so I could inject it into the muscle of their thigh. They didn't seem much worse for the wear, but a couple did manage to turn and viciously bite my glove. With continued practice and experience, this happened with far less frequency.

It was obvious, even early in my career, that the animals did not enjoy the procedures. However, I quickly began to view their injections as a necessary evil that they would just have to endure.

In the same way that pet dogs and cats were uncomfortable getting vaccines and medications and soon recovered from that slight discomfort to forgive me, I imagined that the rats were only mildly annoyed. After all, they didn't (usually) squeak in pain during, or writhe in agony afterward. Mostly, they simply ran to a back corner of their cage when I released them, and turned to face me in the event that I wanted to grab them again. That didn't seem so bad. It didn't occur to me at the time that I really may not be the best judge of another animal's pain.

The experiments were underway. Each study consisted of anywhere from 100 to 150 animals, each cage holding 5 rats, with 10 rats per group. I injected various levels of bovine growth hormone in various formulations and weighed the all animals each day.

All properly designed experiments, in all disciplines of science, require at least one "control" in order to achieve valid results. This helps ensure that any unwanted variables in the experiment are accounted for and thus hopefully eliminated from the analysis. In the context of biomedical research, this often entails one group of animals who do not receive any experimental drug but instead are given a placebo. This way, if there is significant weight gain (for example) in the animals in both the control group and the experimental groups, the researcher can safely rule out their drug as the cause of that weight. Simply put, controls provide a normal baseline against which experiment groups can be compared.

In this study, which wanted to compare not just the effects of the hormone, but also various liposomal methods of delivery, I used two controls. One control was liposomes without any hormone and the other control was simply plain hormone. There was a steady growth in the control animals who received only hormones, differing levels of growth for the different liposome/hormone preparations, and no growth in the controls that received no hormone at all. After thirty days for each study, I compiled the results and plotted them out for comparison in a multitude of colorful graphs and charts. There was no denying how interesting this was. The empirical method. The heart and soul of scientific investigation. But the uglier side of this research was yet to come.

Following the end of each study, I destroyed the animals. They were considered worthless for any additional studies, as they had been both modified by their surgery and also by the hormones given. Even the untreated controls were to be destroyed except for the two I took home as pets. It seemed that I still had a small amount of compassion in me somewhere. I really wanted to bring them all home, rather than kill them, but that was clearly not an option. I honestly think that by saving a couple of them, it helped ease my conscious about the mass murder that I was required to perform. It made it easier for me to turn off the empathy switch, knowing that I could still be a friend to a few.

The rats didn't exactly have a perfect life at my home either. Owning small pets like these was probably a holdover habit from my youth, where my collecting small animals in cages almost verged on hoarding. Once home, however, these little rats lived in the same shoebox cages used in the lab and I never really gave them much enrichment, but at least they lived out their natural lives without pain, and they didn't die in terror.

At a small outfit like Applied Lipids, euthanasia was a rather simple process for rats and mice. It involved a bucket.

After handling these young animals for a full month, they were becoming more docile and friendly each day. They didn't even react too much anymore to the injections, although they certainly became more adept at jumping out of the scale pan. I couldn't help but become rather attached to them. These weren't the strong, giant adult males I'd seen in other cages. These cute little girls were much more like the youngsters I had owned as a child, my dad allowing me to rescue a couple from their fate as food for his snakes. They all had bulging pink eyes and their little pink noses twitched continuously, always smelling the air as if that was how they really viewed the world. In fact, it was. Rats have between five hundred and a thousand different types of olfactory receptors, coded for by a huge number of genes—nearly 1% of their entire DNA is involved in their sense of smell. The amount of information they can learn merely from the smell of each other's urine alone is astounding. Through their noses, they not only can determine the sex of other rats, but also their age, reproductive status, social status, and differentiate between individuals. However, something humans fail to remember is that like most other animals, they can also smell levels of stress. Rats can smell panic, fear, and pain. In addition, they can easily smell death.

The "death bucket," as we called it, was a four-gallon stainless steel pail with a lid that fit loosely on top. A perforated plastic floor rested inside about three quarters of the way down. A few large chunks of dry ice were placed beneath that floor. After I weighed each animal for the final time, I lifted the lid and tossed the rat inside, quickly closing the lid again. The rustling inside the bucket only lasted a minute or so as the little girl thrashed about trying to catch her breath. Dry ice is nothing but frozen carbon dioxide and the bucket held no oxygen as the dry ice sublimated directly from a solid to a deadly gas. The animal was unconscious in less than a minute, although her gasping for air continued on for several minutes longer. They urinated and defecated first as a fear response and again as they died, when their sphincters relaxed. The smell of their waste was noticeable even to my meager human nose and the agitation of subsequent rats waiting to be weighed was obvious. As I removed each rat from the scale, I tossed her into the bucket to join the gasping or already-dead bodies of her cage mates. Her horror and panic must have been tremendous, as she recognized her fate atop the still-warm pile of her dead friends. A large orange biohazard bag was on the floor next to the bucket, as the pail had to be emptied periodically. There were always more dead rats at the end of a study than the bucket could contain. I placed some dry ice into the biohazard bag as well, just in case a few were still alive when I unceremoniously dumped them in.

After a study or two, I decided that the bucket method, while useful for only a few animals at a time, was a bit inefficient for large sacrifices such as these end-of-study kills. Instead, I placed dry ice into the deep sink basin next to the scale and started tossing the rats into the sink. A thick white cloud of the deadly gas rippled as each scared animal fell into its depths. This method also made cleanup much easier, as I didn't have a bucket to wash out, only the sink. I was proud of my creative efficiency, even while feeling some degree of sadness that they all had to die.

I can still feel the warm, heavy softness that a bag full of freshly dead rats felt like as I carried it from the animal facility to the waste storage room. Inside the room, I opened a large fifty-five gallon steel drum that contained other bags with dead animals. I scooped some lime into my bag and then tossed it into the drum, with more lime on top. The lid was sealed until the next bag of animals arrived. On Thursdays, a plain white truck pulled up to the rear door of our building and the smelly drums of corpses were carted off to an unknown incinerator in an unknown location.

This wasn't the first time I had thought about using animals as mere commodities for my own livelihood. Before I started this job, I was renting a room on the second story of a large old farmhouse in rural New Jersey. Without a romantic relationship at the time and no real friends outside of the people I knew at work, I was living as something of a loner. I had recently returned from my brief attempt at college in Kansas (KU had one of the few Occupational Therapy programs in the country at that time) and I was not sure in what direction my life would lead me. My immaturity and lack of vision were evident when I didn't complete the OT program, and coming back to New Jersey was somewhat humiliating. I couldn't return to my parents' home (they were *trying* to empty the nest, as I had always been a handful for them) and this old farm was the least expensive option I could find at the time.

Although the house was quite a few miles away from anywhere and the commute was long, I nevertheless enjoyed the solitude it afforded and the fact that I could walk into the woods and enjoy nature whenever I desired. However, I needed to do something more with my life than simply being a security guard or pet shop clerk. After talking to the homeowner, I decided that this would be a great place to set up a ferret breeding business. Ferrets were quickly becoming a popular pet during the mid-1980s and I felt sure that I could make a lot of money if I bred and sold them. In addition, I would be working with animals, something that I knew I really enjoyed.

I spent several disgusting weeks of my free time shoveling out the five-inch layer of dried guano from the concrete floor of an old chicken coop, wearing a mask and doing my very best not to breath the dust. I was well aware of the many diseases that bird feces carried and I was not at all thrilled about how much work and dust this task involved. Finally, though, I finished and my dad helped me buy and install three sets of six-cage units, formerly used for breeding chinchillas. Once I had mounted these to the walls, I began putting plastic over the open windows to keep the cold out. I realized that I also needed to replace all the screens before spring and repair a leaky part of the roof. As I began to work on restoring functional electric and plumbing, I saw how my expenses were quickly adding up and decided to ask the homeowner if he would help cover the cost of these more expensive and permanent repairs.

I sat down at the kitchen table across from him. "Last week I finally cleaned up all the chicken crap that was in there. That was a lot of work!" I wiped my brow instinctively as I thought of all my sweaty labor. I sat down at the kitchen table across from him.

"I bet it was," he said, finishing the rest of his tuna sandwich. "That place hadn't been used in years."

"I really appreciate your letting me use it. I'm pretty excited to finish getting it set up."

"When do you expect to start breeding?" He was washing his plate in the sink. All the tenants shared the kitchen with him and he was a stickler for cleanliness.

"Probably not until spring," I replied. "I need to finish some repairs and I don't want to buy new animals during the winter." I paused. "I was wondering if you could help with the cost of repairs, however, since these are improvements to your property."

"Well, that wasn't our agreement. I said you could use the chicken coop, but fixing it up was your problem."

"Ok," I mumbled, disappointed. I wasn't sure if I had enough money for the supplies I needed. At least I had all winter to get it done and the fall weather was still nice enough.

He walked over to me. "By the way, I'll need the rent for that building next week."

"What?" I was confused.

"I wasn't charging you rent while you were working on it, but beginning on the first, I'll need an additional hundred dollars per month."

I was shocked. How could this be? I remember specifically asking him a few months prior if I could use the coop for my new breeding business, since it was sitting empty and basically rotting away, unused. He was perfectly fine with that request and never once mentioned any additional rent.

"I thought you said I could use it," I could almost feel my voice wanting to whine. I was far more surprised than angry at this point.

"Yes, you can use it, but not for free. Would I let somebody use my barn without paying for it? Why would the coop be any different?"

Now I was angry. "You never said anything before about rent and yet you let me clean out that whole damned place and do all kinds of repairs to it. I even spent a hundred dollars on plastic to cover the windows for the winter!"

"Well, sorry about that, but it would be silly not to charge you for using one of my buildings."

Three weeks later I moved out of that house, furious. I guess he did me a couple of favors. First of all, he taught me to always get everything in writing. More importantly, however, he kept me from buying a bunch of animals to be bred and sold like so many little disposable toys. Looking back, I'm sure I would have failed at that ambitious endeavor too and perhaps the incomplete execution of my plans meant that a few more lives weren't lost in the process. It took me many years to see that as a silver lining and get over my anger about the whole affair, but in the meantime, most animals were still just commodities in my mind.

Bovine growth hormone was typically injected intramuscular, but the hormone was still rapidly metabolized and cleared from the system, even when encapsulated within liposomes. And so I was introduced to methods of how to perform minor surgery at that time. A new delivery method was going to be tested to see if a large single dose could be given at one time that would still have the desired sustained-release characteristic: implants.

Various combinations of lipids and growth hormone were formulated for testing. More hypox rats were ordered. I anesthetized them using ether in a bell jar, which we called the "opium den." This device looked familiar! This was the same sort of glass jar my dad used when killing insects for his collections, only much larger. About twelve inches tall and ten inches in diameter, this clear container and tight-fitting glass lid also had a perforated floor with wadded-up paper towels underneath. I would pour a couple ounces of ether into the jar, soaking the paper towels with the highly aromatic liquid. I quickly placed a rat inside and watched carefully. There was a small window of opportunity using this method of anesthesia, where too short a duration in the fumes meant that the rat was not fully unconscious and could awaken too quickly, while too long of a duration meant the rat died. One common, industry-standard way to tell if the animal was fully unconscious was to firmly pinch a toe or the tip of the tail between my fingernails and see if there was a response. If she jerked her leg or tail, it meant she was still somewhat conscious and I needed to return her to the ether for a minute more.

Once the animal was knocked out, I removed her and quickly replaced the lid on the jar. I did this swiftly, not only to prevent my own inhalation of the fumes, but also because ether is explosively flammable and a simple static spark could cause quite a bit of damage. The smell of ether is very strong and, despite the lid being closed, the fumes that had permeated the rat's fur were unavoidable. Getting dizzy during extended periods of use was not uncommon for me. My coworkers often commented that using a fume hood was the appropriate safety measure. However, since there were no fume hoods in the animal facilities, the risk was apparently worth it. It wasn't the first or the last time personal safety was ignored in order to facilitate expediency.

I placed the animal on her belly, and soaked her shoulders and neck in ethanol. I did this both to sterilize the incision site and to wet her fur, making the incision much easier to perform. Taking the scruff of the neck in my fingers and pulling the skin up from the shoulder blade, I made an incision about one half-inch-long with a scalpel along the centerline. It was done in this location so that the rat wouldn't be able to easily reach the wound. Taking a different and bladeless scalpel handle from a beaker filled with ethanol (also to keep it sterile), I inserted the round, flat handle end into the incision, separating the skin from the underlying tissue. This was easy, as the skin of most animals is not as firmly attached to the body as you might imagine. The lipid/BST pellet, about the same shape as a dime, but half the diameter, was inserted into this subcutaneous pocket. I then used a surgical stapler to close the incision with a couple of stainless steel staples. Next I applied Superglue, at that time not yet approved for veterinary applications but acceptable for use on rats, to further seal the incision and prevent any leakage. If all went well, I'd return the rat to her cage where she'd recover from the anesthesia in just a few minutes.

Occasionally, the rats would wake up during the procedure, either because I was too slow or because they didn't receive enough ether, or both. In such an event, they would either be returned to the bell jar for more anesthesia, or if they were still groggy enough and I was almost finished, I would complete the procedure on a semi-awake animal. I had a lot of animals to perform this surgery on and I didn't want to postpone my lunch, after all.

No post-operative pain medication was ever given to the rats. Pain management wasn't (and still isn't) considered very important in rodents and is rarely ever used. Because the Animal Welfare Act (AWA) excludes mice, rats, birds, reptiles, amphibians, and most agricultural animals (pigs, cows, sheep, chickens) from any reporting requirements, it's likely that hundreds of thousands of research animals in the US are subjected to painful experiments each year without pain relief. The "Guide for the Care and Use of Laboratory Animals" says that "proper use of animals, including the avoidance or minimization of discomfort, distress, and pain" is to be followed, "when consistent with sound scientific practices." The last part is what allows any institution to treat any animal in any manner they wish without technically violating the AWA—even animals covered under the AWA—as long as they are doing it under the broad and vaguely worded guise of "sound scientific practices." Both the USDA and the AWA are really only interested in proper husbandry in any event, as the law actually only requires that animals receive food, water, vet care, and are housed in clean and safe enclosures that allow them to turn around. Pain and suffering during research is not really a consideration and any violations (if discovered) are often ignored or summarily dismissed with a very small and inconsequential fine.

I later learned that a lot of animals are conscious and awake during their slaughter in meat production. I, like most people, find that to be a horrible scenario—one that is too disturbing to contemplate for long. But how could I consider my hurried surgery on semi-awake animals to be any different? Even at that time, I would have recoiled from the thought of pigs, cows, and chickens being boiled, skinned, or cut apart while alert. What made my actions in the lab seem more acceptable to me?

I think there were a couple of things that made a difference in my mind. One, the procedures were performed in a clean, clinical context with altruistic intentions. This was Science for the Betterment of Humanity, not simple mindless butchery for the taste buds of gluttons. Two, the rats weren't actually being killed at that time. That may not seem like such a large distinction, since they would be killed before long anyway, but the fact that they were meant to recover from the procedure made a difference. Finally, like the people who work in meat-processing plants, I turned off my internal "compassion switch." I was simply doing a job, like a Nazi guard in a concentration camp, following orders. It couldn't be so bad if my supervisor, a well-educated scientist, said to do it.

Right?

It was never really researched whether or not there was actually a market at the time for bovine growth hormone. As it turned out, there wasn't and the research was discontinued. The research group mourned the waste of time and money. Nobody ever mentioned the waste of life.

Applied Lipids had an electron microscope and in those days prior to digital imaging, all photomicrographs had to be developed in our own darkroom. One of my ancillary tasks was to change out the developing solutions as they aged, and, since I entertained the thought of someday becoming a photographer, I looked forward to the day when I would be able to develop my own film. The experience I gained in that darkroom was tantalizing, but not close to what I longed for. Finally, after having worked there for a year, a new study came along that allowed me to develop film and make prints.

This study was to use young "hypox" rats again, this time to study how well, if at all, the epiphyseal plate (growth plate) had fused in the leg bones of animals treated with calcitonin, a hormone involved in the blood's calcium levels and in osteoporosis treatments. The rats who received calcitonin would develop normal joints, while those without treatment would remain in a juvenile (unfused) condition. Various forms of experimental mixtures were tested with varying levels of success.

It was certainly not the first time that I had cut apart an animal, but it was probably the first time I had so clearly looked upon a small animal such as these rats as "meat."

After the end of each experiment, I killed the animals in the "death bucket" and removed one of their rear legs. Removing their legs was pretty straightforward; I made an incision inside the groin using a scalpel, cutting the leg off at the hip joint. I then tossed bodies of the dead into a biohazard bag. Once the leg was detached, I removed the skin and fur, leaving just muscle and bone. Tendons, ligaments, veins, and nerves were all clearly visible and aside from the little furry feet and toes, made me think of the frog legs I had occasionally eaten in Chinese restaurants.

I had enough firsthand exposure to different cultures to realize that what Americans choose as acceptable to eat is not based upon anything other than cultural bias. For example, some Asian cultures eat cats and dogs, while some other cultures eat rats, insects, worms, snakes, etc. Most Western cultures have strong taboos against eating carnivorous mammals, reptiles, and any terrestrial arthropod (such as insects). However, these taboos are not based upon any real biological difference between eating some species and not others (other than the toxicity of a dog's liver compared to a cow's, for example). Those Asian cultures see no ethical or moral difference between a cow and a dog, and in fact, there isn't one. Likewise, Westerners recoil at the thought of eating insects or scorpions, yet we relish eating their arthropod cousins if they come from the ocean in the form of lobsters and crabs.

When I saw the rat legs as meat, it also strongly brought to mind other foods, such as chicken wings, and rabbit, which I had eaten recently as part of a cacciatore (a meal prepared "hunter-style") in an Italian restaurant. Although the irony was lost on me at the time, that meal of similar flesh was a holiday dinner hosted by Applied Lipids. These little rat legs looked no different than any of those other animals and suddenly, as "meat," the tableau of dozens of little legs lined up on plates in front of me didn't seem so gruesome or disgusting. I even ruminated on the fact that because they were fed a wholesome and disease-free laboratory diet, these rats wouldn't be at all harmful for me to eat, compared to wild rats from a landfill or dumpster. I was raised to eat meat as a normal part of life, and emotionally turning my subjects into meat instead of once-living sentient beings almost certainly had the effect of rationalizing my actions.

I placed the legs in neat rows on an eight-and-a-half by eleven sheet of clear plastic normally used for writing on an overhead projector. Carefully, I laid the plastic sheet atop an X-ray cartridge containing the film negative. I placed unique metal identification markers next to each group of legs so I could later identify which experimental group (or control) the legs belonged to. In the room, I had a portable X-ray unit (a big three-foot lead-lined box on wheels) that I used to expose the film. I donned a lead apron and placed a cartridge with its sheet of legs into the box. Pressing a red button resulted in an ominous hum and after the correct exposure time (which I had fine-tuned previously with some "disposable" rat legs), I pressed a green button to stop the X-rays. I then unceremoniously dumped the legs into the bio-bag and prepared the next sheet of legs. I developed the film, printed the images on photography paper, and hung them to dry in the red-lit darkroom. Later, with the help of a pair of calipers, I began the tedious task of measuring the width and thickness of each epiphyseal plate, recording each set of numbers in my notebook as I went along.

Even more than when I was weighing rats, it was during this time when it became clear to me that all the more tedious tasks in any job are relegated to the technicians and other minimum-wage workers. I still felt I was doing important work, but this measurement task was certainly boring, almost as much as performing the statistical analysis on the numbers. I was always interested in seeing the differences between study groups plotted out, though, and I used to enjoy being one of the adepts at using the new computers and software that our lab had purchased. The mid-1980s was an exciting time for personal computing and I was very quickly burgeoning as a computer geek.

As with all living creatures, the variability of individual bodies and their development rates is naturally very high. In order to control for this variability and to get statistically valid results, the number of individuals used for these studies also had to be high. In this case, for each tested compound, I used ten rats per dose level. There were at least two control groups, so a typical experiment used 150 to 200 rats. Dozens of experiments were performed. Thousands of surgically stunted, juvenile rats were literally thrown away.

They were an expendable commodity.

CHAPTER THREE

LD$_{50}$

She was fairly new to the lab, having only worked in a pet store before this. I showed her how to restrain the mice in order to do IP (intraperitoneal) injections in the belly. She seemed to get the hang of it fairly quickly, although there were many times she didn't have the mouse well restrained and she had to let it go before it bit her. She must have become over-confident in her new skill because it wasn't long before she finally did get bit. Her immediate response was to shake her hand violently down, flinging the poor mouse to the floor. Before I could respond, she angrily stomped on the mouse, killing it. She laughed. She never received any disciplinary action. In fact, it was never mentioned again. It was only a mouse, after all.

LD_{50}—median lethal dose. Or as I called it, "counting the dead." More animals have probably been killed by this single experiment model than by any other. Developed in 1927, this test is meant to discover at what dose a compound is lethal in 50% of the animals to whom it is given. In research, it often provides a way for the investigator to narrow in on a dose level that is safe for the subject when exploring a new drug. By knowing the upper dose level that is safe, the researcher can then adjust the dose downward to find the optimum level that is still considered therapeutically effective. LD_{50} is often represented in terms of milligrams of compound per kilograms of body weight and usually reflects an acute (one-time) dose. Thus, the LD_{50} of caffeine in rats is about 192mg/kg. Translated to humans, this is the equivalent of the average adult drinking 100 cups of coffee in one sitting. The problem is, as with most all animal research models, the results of these tests do not translate well to humans. Chocolate, for example, is relatively harmless to humans but highly toxic to many animals. The LD_{50} of theobromide (the toxic compound found in chocolate) in cats is 200mg/kg, while in humans, it's estimated to be about 1000mg/kg. The LD_{50} clearly tells us nothing at all if we were to use it to compare the two species. However, it's standard to use this poison test throughout the food, drug, cosmetic, and chemical industries.

It also meant that I still had a job. Despite the end of the growth hormone studies, there were many other researchers performing studies at this company, and my experience and proficiency with the rats meant I was readily lent out to them—especially for the more routine and standard animal tests that were always being performed. LD_{50} studies were simple but became tedious since I did so many of them over the years. It was also how I began working with mice.

I thought mice were cute, but they were always too small and hyper to make good pets in my mind. They weren't as fun as rats, in other words, and I saw them more as snake food than anything else. Nevertheless, I enjoyed watching them play with each other— loud squeaky wrestling matches and taking turns chasing each other around their small shoebox-sized cages. I also found myself transfixed by watching some of the little creatures perform some fairly elaborate acrobatic maneuvers in their cages. One mouse was particularly adept. He would run from one corner of his shoebox to the diagonal opposite, jump up the wall, do a flip off of the wire lid, then run back to the original corner, where he would do another flip, and repeat the same thing again. This continued for five to ten repetitions before he would stop for a sip of water, nibble on some food, or give himself a tongue-bath, only to begin again afterward. Another mouse simply did continuous backflips off one corner and the lid, over and over and over again. Still others would spin, as if chasing their tail, then reverse direction and do it again. I realized that they did this because they were bored. It was the same kind of behavior one sees in zoos, with animals pacing back and forth behind their bars in a futile attempt to stave off insanity. It was those moments while watching them "play" where I actually took the time to feel a little bad for their situation. I contemplated the fact that they were just grist for the mill and would soon be dead.

Like other laboratory animals, the laboratory mouse was also bred to be docile and easy to work with, but they were nothing like rats. Since they were so much smaller, even handling them took new skills and techniques. Transferring them from cage to cage or from cage to digital scale and back (it seemed I was always weighing animals) was the same—pick them up by the base of their tail. Just like rats, when held this way they could neither turn to bite nor escape. It didn't seem to hurt them any and I was told they didn't mind, but I had no way of knowing if that was true or not. My dad had already warned me long ago not to pick up either rodent by the tip of the tail, as the skin would pull right off. I never tested that theory—it was a pretty gross thought, even for this vivisectionist.

To restrain a mouse for most injections, I would take them by the base of their tail and place them on the metal bars of their cage's lid. Pulling back slightly on their tail would cause them to grab the bars with their forefeet, while I slid the fingers of my other hand up their back. Sliding my finger and thumb down over their shoulders, I would then grab as much scruff of their neck and shoulder skin as I could and lift them up and away from the cage top. If I had enough of the skin held taut, they were unable to turn and bite and since my pinkie-finger of that same hand was also now holding their tail against my palm, they couldn't move their body around either. Their eyes bulged from the sockets with their skin being pulled so tight. I could then tilt their head downward (to allow vital organs to move away from the gut somewhat) and inject them in the belly with whatever compound was prescribed. I injected dozens of mice at one time, in an assembly line fashion and with mindless robotic repetition. Mouse after mouse, only stopping to change needles every five mice or so. The needles became dull fairly quickly and when the point met resistance at their skin, followed by a sudden pop of penetration, I knew that my needle needed changing.

An average LD_{50} study might involve five dose levels and a control. Typically, ten mice would be used for each group, so sixty-two mice would be ordered specifically for this purpose. The two extra mice provided surplus in the event of problems. There weren't often very many problems with the mice, but occasionally one would die during transit from the supplier, or an injection would be botched, etc. It was always better to have extras; mice are cheap. In these kinds of studies with mice, the animals aren't treated as individuals. Their data is comprised more from how they respond as a group, therefore they were not individually tagged and usually not weighed. I followed a fairly straightforward process: When I completed the injections for a group of mice, I returned them to their cage, labeled their cage tag, and made my notebook entries. Then I moved on to the next group.

Each day following the initial injection, I counted the mice. I noted all deaths on the cage tags and in my notebook, removing the bodies promptly upon discovery. Often, the other mice would eat a portion of the dead body if it were left too long. Between the possibility of disease and the chance of more drug being consumed from the flesh, it was important to be prompt about removal. Sometimes the mice would die soon after injection, within hours. Other times it would take many days. Finally, after thirty days had elapsed, the experiment was considered done and I analyzed the results. More often than not, the initial range of doses was off by either too much or too little, resulting in either too many deaths, or too few. A new experiment would then be done with new mice to either broaden the range or adjust it up or down to find the fifty percent lethal dose. This may be done several times and it was not uncommon to go through as many as 250 mice to find the LD_{50}. It was also common that, until that median lethal dose was found, it was impossible for any additional research to continue using that drug.

As with other studies, the untreated controls, while perfectly normal and healthy, were not used for anything else, unless I needed some practice in a new procedure or I needed a normal healthy body part for something else. Usually, I simply destroyed them in the "death bucket" or a foggy sink, along with all the other surviving mice at the end of each study.

Mice are extraordinarily disposable.

CHAPTER FOUR

Hot Rats

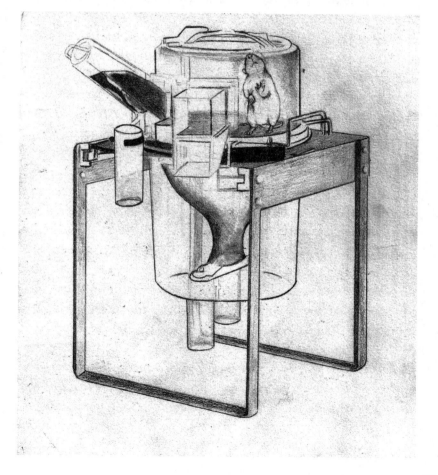

I walked down the hallway connecting the two labs with a Geiger counter in my hand. I was headed back to my bench to scan for the radioactive isotopes I was working with, to be sure that the other "non-hot" areas of my workbench were not contaminated or that the items and areas that I had just decontaminated were sufficiently clean. Normally, I just worked with low-powered ^3H that isn't detectable with this counter, but recently I had been using ^{14}C, a stronger beta emitter. This hallway passed next to our waste room, where both dead animals and radioactive wastes were held, pending pickup. This was also where radioactive isotopes were stored when they weren't being used. The walls were built with a lead liner inside as a precaution against the much stronger gamma emitters and strict procedures and record keeping were in place to protect employees. We each also wore a monitoring badge, which was sent out each month to ensure that we only ever received a safe level of radiation exposure.

As I passed the room, however, the meter on my Geiger counter suddenly squealed and pinned to maximum. The normal tic–tic–tic sound generated by naturally occurring background radiation quickly became a fully insistent and high-pitched buzz. The counter was normally set to the most sensitive level, since I worked with such low-powered isotopes, so I turned the dial to a less sensitive setting and the counter was still pinned at maximum. Turning it all the way down finally brought the counter to a measurable level and it was still reporting an astoundingly high amount of radiation in the hall! I was able to pinpoint the most active region on the wall and it was at a seam where two wall panels met. Something unnerving was going on inside that room. I contacted our safety officer and when I told her about my findings, she immediately investigated. Wearing a lead apron and gloves, she opened the refrigerator on the other side of the wall, near the seam in the hall. On the top shelf, she found four lead bricks that were arranged to form two-inch thick walls around a lead "pig," a cylindrical container made of lead that actually held the isotope. This was the standard method for containing the powerful gamma emitters that a few other people in the lab were using. Someone had forgotten to put the fifth brick, the lid, back on top of the *four walls. Nobody knows (or admitted) how long we had been walking through that hallway unaware of the danger continually bombarding us.*

———————————————————

Radiation! The stuff of nuclear weapons and countless B-grade science fiction movies. I was excited!

Labeling an experimental drug with a radioactive isotope provides the researcher a way with which to determine where, when, and for how long the compound remains in a specific part of the body. In the case of animals I worked with at Applied Lipids, it was either labeled with carbon-14 (^{14}C) or tritium (^{3}H). Again, I was excited at the new and fun things I was learning.

As a boy, I remember my father showing me a few little nuggets of green glass in a small vial. He explained to me how rare they were and also how dangerous. Now, having grown up in a home with plenty of dangerous substances in jars, I wasn't all that concerned. What could a few ugly little greenish boogers do that cyanide couldn't? (Only later, as an adult, did I find out that the impossibly heavy mayonnaise jars full of mercury that I would play with, and the lead bricks and blocks that would be kicking around as weights for various projects, were then-unknown sources of even more danger.) My dad used those green chunks of trinitite and an old radium watch he owned (also dangerous) to teach me about radiation. Trinitite is man-made glass—radioactive sand fused as a result of the plutonium nuclear bomb test performed at the Trinity site in New Mexico. While not nearly as dangerous as he made it sound (it was quite rare and he probably just didn't want me losing any of it), it did help fuel a life-long interest in the effects of radiation, especially as portrayed by Hollywood in the 1940s and '50s.

One of the theoretical benefits of encapsulating drugs into liposomes was their ability to move the drugs to the site of infection or disease. There was also a hope that they could do the opposite in some cases—keep the drug in the location where it was originally injected. Furthermore, testing how long a drug normally stays in the system and where it's anatomically located at certain time points after dosing is also of interest. Enter radioisotope labeling. How it works is that some atoms of carbon or hydrogen in the test compound are replaced with the corresponding isotope (^{14}C or ^{3}H). The less stable isotope functions just the same as the original element, but as it decays, it emits sub-atomic particles that can be detected and measured.

Even though these two isotopes are beta emitters and thus have very low power in their radiation (the energy released during decay won't even pass through a piece of paper), they are still very bio-available and thus dangerous to ingest. All life on Earth is carbon-based, meaning everything we are made of and consume is made with carbon atoms as the central element to the molecular structure. Since the body doesn't differentiate between the stable carbon-12 (^{12}C, which makes up 99% of all carbon on Earth) and the radioactive ^{14}C, it will use either one interchangeably. That means that when ^{14}C is accidentally ingested, inhaled, or absorbed, it will readily become part of our bodies. While the emitted energy is small, at the molecular and cellular level, it can be quite damaging. One way it is most dangerous is by bombarding cellular DNA, changing its structure and potentially causing various cancers; ^{3}H is dangerous in much the same way, except that it replaces stable hydrogen atoms instead of carbon atoms.

In the laboratory, all materials coming in contact with these isotopes (making them "hot") require special handling, labeling, and disposal. Part of my workbench in the main lab had a hot section, which was clearly demarcated with radiation warning tape and a spill tray. Inside this area were all the supplies and instruments that previously had or would soon have contact with radioactive material and they also all had to be labeled with radiation stickers. These items could not be used outside this area and could only be handled with gloves. It was possible to decontaminate them with a special soap, but it was easier to keep hot things labeled as radioactive and reuse them each time they were needed in radiolabeled studies. Contaminated disposable waste products, such as gloves, pipette tips, paper wipes, etc., were disposed of in a special radioactive waste barrel near the biohazardous waste barrels. Careful records were kept each time contaminated material was disposed of and the Nuclear Regulatory Commission was fully involved in every aspect of the use and disposal of our radioactive material. We were even required to send out urine samples on a monthly basis to monitor for any accidental ingestion.

Even though I felt fairly comfortable with all the safety precautions taken by Applied Lipids, I was never fully relaxed when working with radiation. The worst problem for me was that it was invisible. Unlike the radiation of Hollywood, this stuff didn't glow in the dark. Furthermore, the routine swiping and analysis of test strips around the areas of the lab, which were supposedly clean, never made me feel as though others were as careful with hot material as I was (or as I tried to be). If everyone was careful and always cleaned up spills and always labeled every contaminated tool, bench, and beaker, why would there ever be any radiation in "safe" areas? Knowing that the test swipes were just normal routine and NRC-required safety measures didn't ease my mind much either.

I began to feel like I was just being paranoid about it, however. Anytime I expressed my worries, they were laughed off as frivolous.

"Are you sure this is clean?" I asked one of my coworkers, whose workbench was the laboratory version of a landfill. Immediately next to this "clean" bench was his equally cluttered radioactive bench top.

"Of course it's clean," he laughed. "You don't see any radioactive tape on it, do you?" His radioactive workspace was ablaze with the yellow and red tape that warned people of the invisible contamination. Some of the tape was quite old and in many cases, had clearly peeled away over time. Several items in his clean space were also labeled with radioactive tape, even though they should never leave the "hot" space until decontaminated.

I motioned to those misplaced items. "Aren't those radioactive?"

"Not anymore," he said.

"Why are they still labeled with rad tape?"

"Who are you, the NRC?"

Regardless, I needed to borrow this pipetter from him. The tool allowed me to very accurately measure out extremely minute quantities of liquid. I was far from confident that it was uncontaminated though. I thanked him and carried it back to my bench, but not before I donned a pair of gloves. I wasn't going to take his word for it. My supervisor wouldn't buy me a pipetter at this particular volume since it was so rarely needed, so I had to borrow this one.

"Thanks," I mumbled, heading back to my bench.

"Make sure you bring it back clean," he called after me.

I laughed to myself at his uncharacteristic worry over cleanliness and proceeded to decontaminate it on the off chance it was actually radioactive, warning sticker or not. That was always the problem with this stuff: invisibility.

The animals were treated no differently than any other supplies or pieces of equipment that were contaminated. Special precautions had to be taken in every aspect of their use after they were given radioactive compounds. Their cages had to be labeled, handled, and cleaned in a special fashion. Their bedding and waste had to be disposed of in the radioactive waste barrels. In a typical experiment involving a radio-labeled drug given to animals, the normal dosing methods are followed, with the addition of all the extra procedures for dealing with radioactive material. All materials and equipment that ever came in contact with the animals in any way had to be decontaminated or disposed of in the same manner, including bench tops, scales, gloves, syringes, needles . . . and dissection tools.

Sometimes, the animals were housed in metabolic cages for the duration of the study. These were specially designed housing units that allow the researcher to not only monitor the amount of food and water each animal consumes, but also to collect and analyze their waste. Clear plastic cylinders, about twelve inches in diameter (smaller for mice), are clipped into in a special rolling metal rack. Four housing units wide and three rows high, the rack could hold twelve rats, one per plastic container. A plastic lid on top and a steel wire floor within meant that each animal had less than one cubic foot to call home for as long as the study required. Food hoppers and water bottles were attached to the outside of each unit and a waste separator was suspended beneath the wire floor. This separator apparatus was like a funnel, the large opening of which was as big as the entire floor of the metabolic unit. Urine would drip down the sides of the funnel and be collected into a vial with graduations on the side to measure volume. Fecal pellets would fall into another vial. Both vials could easily be removed to study the contents, without disturbing the animal housed above.

Rats and mice are gregarious, meaning they prefer to live in groups, so this solitary confinement was a very stressful environment for them. They were also stressed by living on top of wire screen floors, but as this was not meant for long-term use; the normal (and meager) animal welfare policies regarding housing were not applicable.

Once I dosed the rats with the radio-labeled drug and the appropriate amount of time had passed (often, time-after-dose was one of the variables I tested), I drew blood samples and killed the animals in a specific death bucket used just for radiation-contaminated animals. Depending on where the drug was expected to be, I removed most of their organs, placing each one into its own plastic-capped tube.

An animal has a distinctive smell when its body cavity is opened. As long as the intestines aren't accidentally punctured, it doesn't really smell bad (more of a slightly pungent metallic tang than anything else). The unmistakable smell of blood. This metallic smell is not unexpected, given the amount of iron in blood. Having already dissected animals as a child and teenager, I knew my way around the rat's body fairly well. One or two organs, such as the thymus, were new to me, but for the most part it was very straightforward. Since the heart was no longer beating, there was also very little bleeding, at least not unless I cut into normally bloody organs like the liver or spleen.

In order to determine the level of radioactivity in each organ, and therefore the level of the drug (or its metabolites), a liquid scintillation counter is used. Despite its seemingly lofty purpose to measure radioactivity in hundreds of vials, this is a fairly simple device. The subatomic particles that are emitted by the isotope as it decays transfer energy to fluorescing molecules in the "cocktail" that the sample has been put into. This energy dislodges photons (light particles) in the cocktail, which the machine then detects and measures. The resulting value is provided as the raw data used to compare between samples. However, I did not simply drop a rat spleen into a scintillation vial and put it into the machine. Because the samples have to be completely clear in order to not block the photons being emitted, they have to be processed first.

One of the more distasteful tasks I had in the lab was processing the organs that I harvested from radioactive rats. This involved several steps for each organ, utilizing many tubes and vials. First, I had to cut and weigh pieces of each organ so all samples of each type of organ were consistent in size. Next, I measured and added a specific amount of de-ionized water and liquefied the tissue with an ultra hi-speed device, called a tissue homogenizer. This has rotating blades within a hollow probe that shears tissues at the cellular level, producing a similar result as an ultra-efficient precision blender. The device was deafeningly loud at high frequencies and required earplugs as well as a mask because there was a certain amount of aerosolization of the radioactive mixture. I and others jokingly referred to the resulting pinkish muck as a "rat shake" for its milkshake-like appearance and consistency. I then took a small measured sample, just a few drops, of this cloudy mix from the original plastic tube and placed it into a glass scintillation vial. In order to be sure that the final liquid was perfectly clear, it had to be digested. I added small amounts of concentrated hydrogen peroxide and perchloric acid to the vial and placed it, along with all the other vials of homogenized organ samples, into a small oven under a fume hood. This highly reactive mixture, its chemical digestion further fueled by heat, resulted in nothing remaining in the vial the next day but a small amount of clear liquid. Finally, I added a commercially prepared scintillation cocktail, filling up the vial. All of this was done with the many cumbersome extra precautions and contamination controls for radioactivity in place.

Others often reminded me in the lab that the fume hood I used (the only one available to me) was not rated for perchloric acid use. The problem is that as the acid is cooked off from the vials, it's captured in the hood's filters and builds up over time. This particular acid is the strongest commonly used acid (often labs are not permitted to store more than one pound at a time, although we did) and it is highly reactive, especially when heat is applied. While that is good for tissue digestion, the oxidized salts that form in the hood over time are extremely shock sensitive and highly flammable. A hood not rated for perchloric acid could potentially explode without warning and with disastrous results. I was told by my supervisors not to worry about it, but I did.

Working with invisible isotopes in this manner wasn't the fun stuff of science fiction that I had always imagined. It was mostly a pain in the ass and made me constantly fearful of becoming contaminated. Since the most likely result of any such contamination might be developing cancer many years or decades later, I will never be able to tell for sure if it came from this job or not.

All I could do was be careful and cross my fingers.

CHAPTER FIVE

Force-Fed and Soapy Feet

The basket on the three-beam balance in which I weighed rats was a circular affair, much like a small stew pot, stamped out of thin sheet metal with numerous half-inch holes stamped through the side. There was nothing polished or smooth about it, simply dull gray steel with a lid. However, it became obvious to me after using it for a while that the rats were being injured by it. I was always careful to lift them safely by the base of the tail, but nonetheless they grabbed onto whatever they could in order to not be removed from the perceived safety they were in, whether it was their cage or the scale basket. They always managed to grab onto the edges of the holes punched into the basket. I would pull them firmly and steadily until they let go, just as I did whenever they managed to hold onto anything else while being lifted. What I didn't notice at first, until I saw the blood, was that the relatively sharp edges of those holes were pulling their toenails loose. But since I couldn't do anything about it (they had to be weighed, after all), I continued putting them into the basket, getting their weight, and removing them, each time causing them certain pain and distress.

By far, the longest-lasting and most in-depth research I performed at Applied Lipids was that involving NSAIDs (Non-Steroidal Anti-Inflammatory Drugs). Most NSAIDs are very effective at reducing both inflammation and pain and most of us use these compounds fairly regularly, usually in the form of over-the-counter aspirin, ibuprofen, or naproxen. All of them also have a major drawback, however—irritation and bleeding of the gastrointestinal tract. At the time I worked there, one of the most effective NSAIDs for the treatment of fever, pain, stiffness, and swelling was the prescription drug indomethacin. It was also one of the most bothersome because of the gastric side effects—particularly severe ulceration of the stomach and intestine.

The main focus of my research was, like many projects at Applied Lipids, to reduce toxicity while maintaining or even enhancing effectiveness. Using liposome technology to do this with indomethacin (and perhaps other NSAIDs) was very promising and potentially lucrative for the new startup. First, however, we needed a model to measure the relative effectiveness of the drug being used. Since pain cannot be measured in lab animals (and is still a very subjective and hard to quantify aspect in humans), one of the best ways to measure whether this drug was still as effective in our new formulations was by measuring how well it reduced swelling.

As with all animal studies, the larger the quantity of animals used, the more accurate the results. But measuring swelling was not a simple procedure, especially when large numbers of animals were required. Enter the plethysmometer. The name of this device was almost as much fun to pronounce as the instrument itself was to use. Except for one aspect, it was painless for the animal. However, it provided a source of amusement for others in the lab, as I became an expert on how to use (and pronounce) this rather obscure and almost comical contraption.

It was indeed a contraption. Following assembly instructions, the result resembled something invented by a seven year old with an Erector Set more than anything else. A vertical metal rod, two feet long and affixed to a heavy base, supported a soda can-shaped reservoir and a rectangular, clear acrylic cube. This cube had various wires, tubes, and holes, none of which made any sense at first glance. This was how I was going to measure rats? The cube featured two hollow cylindrical wells, arranged side-by-side, the one closest to the front being open at the top. The hollow wells were each about the size and shape of a roll of quarters and were connected to each other only by a small tubular opening near the bottom. A couple of wires attached to the rear of the cube connected to a black electronic box that was plugged into an AC outlet. Another wire went from the box to a foot switch on the floor. A couple of translucent lines etched into the wells marked the operational range for the device, it was explained, as I poured special soapy water into the reservoir and turned a valve to fill the cylinder with the open top. The open tube between the wells allowed the water level to equalize and when the level was near the lower of the two lines, I closed the valve. The device was now ready to use.

I turned the box on, and other than the power switch it had only one other button. A four-digit numeric display on the front was the only feature showing any activity from this device, as its bright red numbers slowly increased and decreased before finally stabilizing. When the solitary button on top was then pressed, the numbers changed to all zeros. I decided to test it by drawing a line on my finger and then inserting my finger into the liquid in the open well, up to the line. As I did so, the numbers jumped. Holding my finger still (the numbers still seemed to jump around a bit), I stepped on the floor switch. That froze the numbers on the display. I withdrew my finger and pressed the button on top again, and again it showed all zeros. Archimedes would have been proud! This device measured the amount of liquid displaced by an object inserted into the open well. The volume level was measured using detectors mounted within the attached, but sealed well.

But what about the animals? In order to test swelling reduction, edema had to be induced in the rats first. This was accomplished by injecting carrageenan into the pads of their feet. Carrageenan is a gelatinous substance extracted from seaweed. It has been used as a food additive since the Middle Ages and has generated some controversy recently regarding possible negative health effects upon ingestion. When it is injected into animals, inflammation and swelling is one major result. The rat model functioned like this: I injected carrageenan into the pad of their left rear foot, causing severe swelling of that foot by the next day. Typically, the foot would swell to two or three times its normal size. I then took measurements of both rear feet with the plethysmometer, the untreated foot serving as a normal control. By using the untreated foot as a control for each animal, all variability between animals was eliminated. An absolute edema value for each rat could be derived by simply subtracting the normal foot measurement from the swollen foot measurement. The relative reduction of swelling over time could then be determined when groups of animals given various preparations of NSAIDs were compared, both to each other and to fully untreated controls.

The water was soapy to eliminate surface tension, thus ensuring complete wetting of the rat's foot and eliminating air pockets that would skew the data. In order to achieve consistent results for the duration of each study and from animal to animal, their foot must also be dipped into the well to the exact same depth each time. The recommended method for ensuring this is to tattoo a line on their ankle, to which the water level is measured when hitting the foot switch. For once, I seemed to have the welfare of the animal in mind when I suggested to my supervisor that we first try using a permanent marker to draw a line (and touch it up as required). If that didn't prove satisfactory, we could then resort to tattoos. As it worked out, the drawn line was very adequate. This was another hint of compassion peeking through my analytical mind.

I found it hard to believe that such extremely specialized equipment was actually being made for such a specific laboratory use. Surely, we were one of just a very small handful of labs that used this contraption. Was there really a large enough market for plethysmometers to justify the manufacture of these things? Little did I realize then how large the laboratory animal industry actually was. That perspective dramatically changed when I was sent to a conference in Philadelphia.

The event was huge. Renting out the city's entire convention center, the American Association for Laboratory Animal Science (AALAS) held its annual conference and trade show over the course of several days. There were many workshops, lectures, panel discussions, and seminars spread out in countless conference rooms and small auditoriums, each and every one dedicated to the topic of doing experiments on animals. A large directory listed and described each subject and I had to choose those that were of interest to me in such a way as not to miss others that my supervisor felt were more important. There were more events than I had time for and I couldn't be in two places at once. It was somewhat overwhelming. Attendees were usually not primary investigators, as I had originally expected. This convention (and the organization itself) was focused almost entirely upon the lab worker—people like me who actually did the hands-on work with the animals.

In addition to the dozens of topic discussions available, the entire lower floor of the facility was also filled with noisy and colorful booths from research device manufacturers; chemical supply companies; mouse, rat, and dog breeders; monkey suppliers; and other industry representatives. There were hundreds of companies there, both small and large. For example, one booth might be showing off their most delicate brain electrodes (suitable for everything from horses to fish), while next to them a two-person company could be stationed offering tasty samples of cat treats, both of whom were across the aisle from a large breeder promising the very best genetically engineered mice in existence. Free handouts of toys featuring cute animals emblazoned with a company's logo filled the large plastic bags I carried, competing for space with the reams of product literature that were forced into my hand at every step. A pretty young woman dressed in a cute fluffy rat costume walked around the convention floor, handing out buttons that said, "Don't get your whiskers in a twist, buy all your quality rats from us. We're head and tails above the rest."

This was serious business. BIG business. All the thick catalogs from these companies that I ordered supplies from back at my lab and all the ads I used to peruse in the AALAS magazine didn't come as close as this convention did to make me realize just how immense the animal research industry was.

So how does one give orally administered drugs such as indomethacin to rats? Most drugs have a bad taste, often bitter. This is especially true for NSAIDs (familiar to anyone who has tasted aspirin) and therefore, one can't simply mix the drug into their food. Furthermore, a precise quantity of any drug must always be delivered and this is most easily controlled by direct oral dosing.

Long ago, scientists discovered that rats also have a physiological peculiarity that is both their blessing (as a species) and their curse (as individuals): they cannot vomit.

As a species with an incredibly high reproductive rate, this inability to vomit is highly beneficial in the long run. Imagine a few wild rats stranded on debris who are swept away by a tsunami onto an island where no rats had existed before. An island filled with new plants, fungi, and insects that they are not familiar with. When they ingest various poisons and toxins from the strange food in their new environment, and being unable to vomit, many of them may die. But the few who live, because they happen to possess a mutant genetic immunity to those toxins, go on to reproduce, passing this immunity trait on to some of their offspring. Because they breed so prolifically (and because the toxins in our hypothetical scenario kill all those without the trait), the trait quickly becomes widespread, eventually affording immunity to the entire species on that island. Unfortunately, this inability to vomit has also contributed greatly to the use of the rat in laboratories, where they can be force-fed any number of experimental compounds, the researcher being confident that the full amount given will stay within the rat's stomach.

The gavage tube is a slightly bent stainless steel tube that is affixed to a syringe in place of an injection needle. Instead of a sharp point, the end of the tube is terminated with a small, perforated ball, so the whole tube passes smoothly through the mouth, into the esophagus, and finally into the stomach before liquid is passed through the tube. Gavage tubes for rats are typically two to three inches long and for mice about half that length and half the diameter.

The rat is held as described before and the ball of the tube is placed into their mouth. Their first response is to bite, but they soon give up on that, as the metal doesn't yield to this attack. When the ball is placed to the back of their mouth towards the roof, it can then be slid fairly easily into the esophagus and down to the stomach. Any resistance encountered means that you likely entered the trachea by accident and you must withdraw and try again. Injecting liquids into the lungs is often fatal. I learned the hard way how miserable that looks, as the rats gasp for air and bloody foam comes out of their mouth. Again, some form of compassion must have existed in me, as I never wanted to do that again. Of course, it also meant a wasted research subject, something to avoid. The whole process generally only took a few seconds after some experience, something I gained quickly.

Other than for the determination of an LD_{50}, giving oral doses to mice was not done very frequently, as the bulk of the studies I did on NSAIDs only involved rats. This was a good thing because it was far too easy to enter the lungs of mice. If you push too hard (because the resistance is not as noticeable in mice), it's also easy to puncture their lungs. This is compounded by the fact that the stomach is located below the lungs and, normally, insertion must be done to the full length of the gavage needle. This detail was not a textbook lesson, and like most of the lessons involving animal research, I learned about what not to do the hard way. I really despised when an error on my part resulted in the unnecessary suffering and death of an animal. I wasn't there to torture animals; I was there to simply use them to reach our humanitarian (and profit) goals. Most people, including me, don't want to be confronted with the negative aspects of their job.

It's well established that when people are placed in uncomfortably negative situations, they will frequently resort to dark humor as a coping mechanism to help relieve some of the heaviness that surrounds them. While this is often helpful, sometimes it goes a little bit over the top.

I was always known as being sarcastic, full of bad puns, and something of a smart-ass. I loved irreverent humor and was always seeking ways to poke fun at established traditions and institutions. George Carlin was a favorite comedian of mine and nothing was off-limits, as far as I was concerned. I probably should have reigned it in a bit one Halloween.

The company Halloween party wasn't ever an official event, as the company's lawyer was very quick to point out. We all wanted to have booze and the company wanted none of the liability, so it was held at the home of one of the research directors. Costumes were mandatory and this year I wasn't going to be outdone. I bought a four-foot-long dowel and painted it white, with a two-inch red tip. Dressed head to toe completely in white, I donned a pair of sunglasses, a pair of rabbit ears, and a partial mask made of rubber that gave me a rabbit's nose, whiskers, and buck teeth. To make the horrible image complete, I cut a hole into the bottom of a large orange biohazard bag. I slipped this bag over my body and popped my head through the hole. Placing my arms through holes on the sides and tapping my cane as I walked, I was now a research rabbit, blind and discarded.

I thought it was funny at the time, as did some of my coworkers, but my recollection is that many of the others at the party were only nervously laughing or even scowling at the image. I can only imagine what some of their spouses thought. Hindsight is twenty-twenty, of course, and I'm now ashamed of what I wore, but even at that time I realized that the sort of indifference I exhibited towards the plight of these animals was making a lot of people uncomfortable. If only I knew then what I know now; their discomfort should have been a clue to me that my levels of empathy were sorely lacking. Unfortunately, this was not the last time that I would take dark humor about my work too far.

CHAPTER SIX

Ulcers

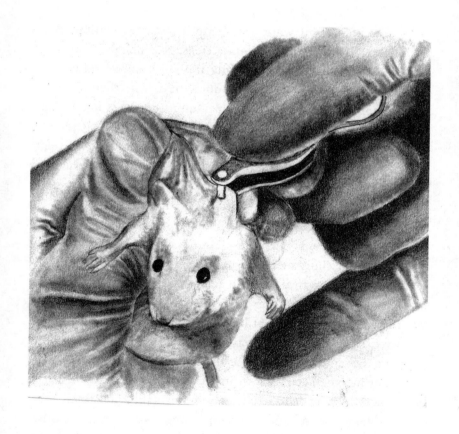

A day didn't go by where I didn't hear a bacon joke or have somebody hold their nose and wrinkle their face when they passed by me at my bench. The strips of small intestine, cut into segments, slit open lengthwise and spread flat did look like bacon. The severe trauma and necrosis present in the samples smelled worse than nearly anything else imaginable. It was the smell of rotten flesh combined with partially digested fecal matter, bile, mucus, and blood. I was hunched over tray after tray of this stench, eight hours at a time. I rarely ate lunch on those days. This was my life two or three days a week for several years. Science!

The bulk of my work was measuring the devastation caused by indomethacin to the gastrointestinal tract of rats. Or, to put it more accurately, I was measuring the devastation and extreme agony *I* caused to rats by forcing indomethacin into their GI tracts. Plethysmometry allowed for the measurement of an anti-inflammatory drug's effectiveness and to ensure that potential candidates for a liposome-encapsulated NSAID would remain useful in treatment. However, the primary goal of our research was to reduce the ulcerative side effects of NSAIDs. Like all such studies, the method involves inducing the toxicity. This was going to get ugly.

The use of indomethacin by humans is well known for causing gastric ulcers as a side effect. This is true of most all NSAIDs, but since indomethacin is cheap, off-patent, and was (at that time) commonly prescribed to treat the pain and inflammation associated with osteoarthritis, it was our drug of choice to experiment with. As with all drug studies, there were at least two control groups, positive and negative. The negative control was treated the same as all other groups, receiving the same formulations as the study groups, except that there wasn't any indomethacin. The positive control received indomethacin, but without it being delivered in an experimental formulation.

The number of animals used per study was often, as in other rodent studies, large. A single formulation, administered with (for example) five different levels of indomethacin, was compared to controls, with one negative control group and also a positive control group for each level. This meant that, with each group consisting of 10 rats, there were 110 animals used. There was one negative control group (10 animals), 5 formulations of different drug levels (5 x 10 = 50 animals), and positive controls at those same levels (5 x 10 = 50 animals). I performed many studies of this size, as there were many different formulations to test. In addition, not only was the drug dose being tested, but the basic methods to best study the gastric effects of the drug were also explored. This meant that different routes of administration (oral versus sub-cutaneous), different organs (stomach versus intestine), and different dose regimens (acute versus chronic) all were dealt with in various ways. Each new variable required their own studies—and required more animals.

For example, since indomethacin was usually administered to humans in an oral dose, this was the most logical way to study it in rats. However, giving the drug via a sub-cutaneous route was also examined to evaluate if this was a comparable method. Giving an injection under the skin requires pulling the skin away from the animal's body, usually above the shoulders near the neck, forming a "tent." The needle is then inserted through the skin into the hollow of this tent. This is the same method used to deliver subcutaneous injections in many animals, including dogs and cats. This delivery method was ultimately not used very much for our research. The wasted lives of those animals were only measured in terms of their financial cost, however.

The first path of investigation focused on the stomach. Eighteen to twenty-four hours prior to dosing, I removed all food from young male rat's cages. Rats and mice are nocturnal, so they spent their last night of activity in a state of hunger. The next day, I gave the rats their oral dose, either a study formulation or one of the controls. Four hours later, I killed the animals in the death bucket, one group at a time. I sat in the animal room, the stench of their urine and feces wafting through the air as their bowels relaxed at death. As I waited for them to die, I could hear the kicking of their feet and legs against the sides of the bucket—their last feeble and reflexive attempts to escape from the misery and doom they were facing. The lifelessness of their eyes was often the easiest way to determine that they were indeed dead, as I placed them on the paper bench top liner, one next to the other, belly-up, as if in an assembly line. When spraying down their bellies with ethanol, occasionally one would start to wake up. This was especially true if the amount of dry ice had gone low and the amount of time to die was misjudged. In that case, I returned the rat to the bucket to finish dying while I processed the others. The rat stomach, being empty, was fairly small—about the size of a nickel. I removed it, cut it open, rinsed it in saline, and placed it into a labeled tube along with the other stomachs from his group. Group after group, animal after animal, stomach after stomach. No thinking involved—just kill, spray, remove, cut, rinse, repeat, then grab the next cage of frightened animals and do it again. I was an automaton of organ removal. Empty cages were stacked along the wall. Tray upon tray of stomach-filled tubes were taken into the walk-in cold room to await my examination. Large orange bags filled with the disemboweled dead piled up in the corner, waiting to be taken to the lime barrels. Another day at the office.

Using a dissecting microscope with a micrometer eyepiece, I spent the entire next day hunched over stomachs floating in cold saline. I examined a parade of little rat stomachs. When laid open, they resembled small wet butterflies. The wrinkly, pink, mucosal surface was facing up and lesions often appeared as contrasting black areas, black because of blood in the ulcer. In the negative controls, there were never any ulcers. In the positive and higher-dose groups, however, the ulceration was often significant—20, 40, even 60% of the stomach's surface area being fully ulcerated was typical in these studies. Writing down the measurements of the ulcers generated the data that I would later analyze for comparison. I rarely thought about how much pain they must have felt with this amount of injury. Even small ulcers give humans a great deal of discomfort. Yet, when you walk into a rat room during the day, they are usually sleeping whether sick or not, so you cannot get a feel for any discomfort. This inability for humans to judge pain in animals was one major reason it became so commonplace to use them in research and was probably one of the reasons I was able to sleep at night, despite the work I was doing.

In a series of side studies, we decided to determine if the lipids used to make liposomes would also decrease the likelihood of ulcerous lesions caused by ethyl alcohol. Instead of oral indomethacin, the rats were force-fed a large amount of grain alcohol as their injury inducement. Unlike indomethacin, this must have been immediately excruciating for them, as the burning pain of alcohol is well known to anyone who has taken a shot of hard liquor on an empty stomach. As with indomethacin, the resulting ulcers were also quite severe. The only silver lining, if there was one, is that the drunkenness that they experienced probably also numbed some of their pain before they died.

The stomach ulcer studies were acute, single-dose studies. More harrowing was when I began doing chronic intestinal studies, where the rats would receive a dose every day for fourteen days. If the stomach ulcers were bad, the resulting carnage to their intestines from these studies was simply horrific.

This work was quickly becoming tedious. Hundreds of rats, hundreds of stomachs, hundreds of hours hunched over a microscope. Dish after dish of stomachs floating in saline, speckled (or worse) with the black spots of ulceration, all measured and disposed of. In the beginning, I had to use the micrometer built into the microscope's eyepiece to measure the length and width of each ulcer, writing the numbers down in my notebook. I generated columns and columns of numbers, which I dutifully entered into a computer for statistical analysis and plotting. Eventually, it was decided that we needed more accuracy, so I was given a set of digital calipers. The new tool didn't break the monotony, however, and it was all I could do to keep on the task and not find some other distractions in the lab to keep me entertained. I was bored, but my coworkers were always a source of entertainment.

This was the first time that I had every worked with people my age who were professionals. I was in my mid-twenties, but all my jobs prior to this had been minimum wage positions that required little education or experience. Before this, I had worked in delicatessens, convenience stores, pizza shops, apartment maintenance, landscaping, home healthcare, and even in a daycare center. However, this was the first time I worked with people who had nearly all graduated with at least a bachelor's degree in biology or chemistry, and most had attained or were working toward a graduate degree. I definitely felt as though I was near the bottom of the totem pole, even though nobody ever made me feel that way. While I'm no longer obsessed with status, at the time I was glad that at least the two animal caretakers who worked there cleaning cages were at or below my level of education. I was smugly aware that I was more of a scientist than either of them and certainly more of one than our company's receptionist. I didn't treat them as beneath me in any way, but it did give me some internal satisfaction knowing that I wasn't the lowest of the low.

Most of the other researchers were in their thirties and their offices were like playgrounds from my perspective. While I was given a desk space in the lab, they were working in rooms of five or six desks, where there always seemed to be a party going on. Walking by one of these rooms at any given moment, I could hear peals of laughter and other indications of non-work-related hijinks from within. I found myself trying to join in, but more often than not, I wasn't really accepted as one of them. They were all nice to me, but I could tell that I really didn't belong. I assumed then (and now) that it was because I was seen as just some kid the company hired to handle rats and their organs. After all, I wasn't writing any research papers or presenting posters at various conferences. I wasn't even the person presenting my data to our own management. While I didn't entirely fit in with those cliques, I did make a lot of friends with several of the other researchers and overall felt fairly happy working there.

It was an exciting time in the biotechnology industry. There were hundreds of startups popping up all over, in the hopes of getting rich quickly off new advances in the biotech world, with companies like Genentech showing how each of us could all soon be millionaires. Our company was no different, and a big part of the thrill of working there was the fact that I was given generous stock options and we were going to go public! As it was, the biotech bubble eventually burst and I never did make much money from my stock options, although management did profit quite well. My job was to find more profit through the results of my animal studies.

The doses were lower for the fourteen-day intestine studies than they were for the stomach studies, but their cumulative effect was far greater. While this spared the stomachs from getting ulcers (for the most part), the intestines were heavily affected. The dosing followed the same protocol as before, but instead of being fasted, the rats were allowed to eat as normal. At the end of the study, instead of removing just the stomach, the entire length of small intestine was removed as well.

Upon exposure to the cool air, the intestines writhed and squirmed about on their own. This is a natural reflex that remains for a short time after death. It was a rather creepy sight the first time I witnessed it and I never really got used to it. Surprisingly, for an animal that fits in your hand, the length of their small intestine is about three feet long! It came out of the rat easily enough. I was pulling it away from the mesentery in one long piece—a slimy, slippery tube. Because the animals were fasted the night before they were to be killed, the intestines were nearly empty. Once the stomach and small intestine were completely removed, I would stick the nozzle of a squirt bottle into one end and squirt saline through the intestine, flushing out bile and any other matter that remained, finally squeezing it out the other end. The rats were fed an herbivorous diet, so any food remaining in their GI tract was not horribly smelly. The entire intestine would then go into a labeled tube, filled with saline, and refrigerated. Harvesting these intestines was a somewhat messy task but not too terribly unpleasant.

It was easy and not too noxious, that is, with the rats who received the lower doses or who were in the negative control group. However, the rats who were given very high doses or were in the positive control group were an entirely different matter. Never before in my life had I experienced the odors that came from the body cavity of those poor souls. Immediately upon cutting into their belly, the smell would hit you. These animals were rotting from the inside out. The smell of their necrotic tissue was much worse than odors you might encounter elsewhere, such as a dumpster or sewer. Much of the nauseous smell came from putrescine and cadaverine, two organic compounds that are created by putrefying flesh. The worst of these mutilated intestines were also knotted and scarred, twisted into tight, dense masses that made it very difficult to extract. In addition, the membranes of these normally tough organs also had so many perforations and thinned areas, it was impossible to pull it out in one piece. It had to be cut out in sections and rinsed carefully. If any of the slimy black matter from inside the intestine came in contact with your skin or clothes, you would smell like that for the rest of the day. As it was, I had to keep a separate lab coat in the room for that work because it retained so much of the odor, even absorbing it directly from the air.

It was not uncommon for the most severely affected animals to die from the destruction to their intestines before it was time to harvest their tissues. Typically, they would have stopped eating, but it wasn't starvation that finally killed them. They died from massive internal bleeding into their gut due to their perforated intestines. I now have a hard time comprehending the immense pain they must have endured. Death was probably a welcome relief. At the time, I was more disgusted by the smell of their emaciated, bony bodies when I had to retrieve them from the cage. I was also worried that the data would suffer from not having a large enough sample size. These are not unusual thoughts that occur to a vivisectionist as they collect their dead.

Because of the often disgusting and time-consuming task of their removal, I'd usually examine all the intestines the next day. The relatively healthy ones were easy to lay out on twelve by twelve inch acrylic trays lined with blotter paper. I cut to length a dozen strips of each intestine and laid them out side by side, one animal per tray. I stacked the trays ten-high next to my microscope and went over them one at a time. When I finished one stack, I retrieved another from the walk-in cold room.

The cold room was very much like what you might find in the back of a restaurant, and in fact may very well have been one originally designed for that more innocuous purpose. However, in addition to the temporary storage of my animal tissues, this one held innumerable vials, tubes, buckets, boxes, bags, and flasks of perishable chemicals, experimental compounds, and other supplies used by the rest of lab. My tissues were not the only ones in there either. Dozens of other researchers' vials containing rabbit eyeballs or less identifiable pieces of animals were also stored there for future analysis.

Measuring the ulcers was pretty straightforward on the healthier samples. The horribly destroyed tissues, on the other hand, were not so easy to measure. In fact, in the worst samples, the term "TMTC" (too many to count) was often entered as the measurement. The stench of those tissues filled the entire lab, much to all of my coworkers' frequently voiced dismay.

I used to have bad intestinal cramps while I was working there, probably from undiagnosed irritable bowel syndrome. Those cramps were some of the worst pain I ever experienced and looking back, I can't help but wonder if my body was more in tune with my horrible actions than my conscious brain acknowledged. The irony is that even though I was suffering from intestinal pain, I never really saw the rats as suffering too much from the torture I inflicted upon their intestines.

Occasionally, someone would walk by and say to me, "Those poor rats."

I would respond, "Yeah. . . ." and then the subject would change. Getting back to work, I didn't think much more about it.

Indomethacin is not prescribed as much anymore. There are newer, more tolerable medications now. Like all the animal studies I performed, these too would prove to be a waste of time, money, and most importantly, innocent lives.

At one point during this time, Vice President George H. W. Bush paid us a visit on his tour of the many new biotech companies that were beginning to pop up across the nation. The entire lab had been fully screened for bombs by the Secret Service, although I was quite amused that they never checked inside the large centrifuges—a seemingly obvious place to hide them. All the employees that wished to be there that day had to undergo background checks. I honestly thought that I would be asked to stay home, since I was fascinated by Russia and was a subscriber to *Soviet Life* magazine. I was certain that I had an FBI file as a result. One of our chemists from Canada was asked by his supervisor to stay home, as his immigrant status in the US was highly questionable. I thought it was funny at the time, but I was strictly informed that I would not, under any circumstance, be doing smelly and disgusting intestine measurements while Bush was there. Nevertheless, it made the local news and I felt like I had my fifteen minutes of fame when I saw myself on local television, looking at absolutely nothing through an unplugged and dark microscope. The Vice President wasn't the only high-profile visitor either. It seemed that this company was always staging "dog and pony shows" in an attempt to drum up capital investment.

It seems strange that my participation in so much torture didn't create much turmoil for me, emotionally or otherwise. All of my friends at that time were also the same people who worked in the lab, so it was just business as usual as far as we were concerned. It was a job and nothing more.

I remember one time as a child, I felt bad when my dad poisoned a colony of ants.

"What are you doing?" I asked.

"I'm killing this ant colony." It seemed to him that what he was doing was plainly obvious.

"Why?"

"Because they are too close to the house and we don't want them here."

"Can't you move them?"

"No, because they all stay with their queen and she's too far underground to reach."

"We can't dig her out?" I was looking for an alternative. I always liked ants and I would spend hours on my belly watching them bustle about in their silent non-stop labor.

"No, I'm afraid not," he replied patiently, quite used to me asking questions.

I watched as he spread the colorful and dusty crumbles of poison around the anthill. I didn't think it was right for him to destroy such a large number of animals, and told him so.

He laughed. "Look at it this way. What I am doing is acting as a force of nature and this is going to result in the evolution of ants." He was shifting fully into teacher mode now. "By killing this colony, and thus preventing it from creating more new colonies near the house, I am putting selective pressure upon the species and helping future ant colonies be more successful *away* from the house, helping them evolve to a type of ant who would naturally want to stay away from humans."

I didn't really understand any of this at the time. He always made a lot of sense and would pride himself on his critical thinking skills and logical mind (*Star Trek's* "Mr. Spock" was a true hero to him). He always knew what he was talking about and I only had a basic grasp of evolution at the time, but I simply felt that, whatever his explanation, it was a mean thing to do to all those ants. The next day, I poked around with a stick at all the little ant bodies that were lying about the now-deserted hill, feeling sad.

Why didn't that same feeling arise again years later when I thought about the lives I was destroying in the lab? Was it really just because my innocent, youthful naivety had dissolved, or was it symptomatic of a larger, more callous disregard for life, reinforced by some legendary promise of Scientific Progress?

I was acutely aware of the numbers of animals I destroyed, but they were just rats and mice. Presumably, they possessed simple minds without much knowledge or concern of their surroundings. It's not like I was doing research on humans, monkeys, or even dogs.

CHAPTER SEVEN

Dogs

This dog was slowly starving to death. Frail and emaciated, his toothpick legs and clearly defined ribs and vertebra were visible under his baggy skin. He had received the highest dose of indomethacin and the ulcerative side effects prevented him from absorbing any nutrients from his food (not that he had an appetite anymore anyway). From my experience with rats, I knew that his intestines were fully destroyed. I also realized for the first time that all these animals, dogs and rats alike, were suffering excruciating pain. Barely able to stand up, he still tried wobbling to the front of the cage to greet me but fell onto his face instead. Lying there with his eyes never leaving mine, he was still rapidly wagging his tail at the sight of me. I was purposefully killing him slowly and painfully and yet he was so very happy to see me.

Our rat studies had shown some promise, so the next step was to move to another species, presumably closer to humans than rats are. Dogs have very sensitive GI tracts, so a dog model was chosen as the next step. Since Applied Lipids didn't have dog facilities, we contracted the study to a laboratory dog breeder in Wisconsin. They specialized in breeding genetically pure strains of dogs, as well as mixed breeds for their customers that desired a more diverse background. Contrary to popular belief, dogs are not stolen off the street or frequently taken from pounds for use in animal research. It's simply much cleaner, safer, cheaper, and more controlled to buy animals from these very clinical and controlled puppy mills. They are the research equivalent of factory farms designed for meat production. I didn't get a chance to see the breeding facility, and in hindsight I'm glad. Instead, I was sent there to review the animals that we contracted the breeder to dose on our behalf.

As with most dog studies in biomedical research, beagles are the breed of choice. In our study, males were used exclusively. This is often done because males don't have a heat cycle (estrous), which interferes with long-term studies. In addition, a female's fluctuating hormones are usually considered an unwanted variable. Females also have more value as breeders and thus males are cheaper—and relatively disposable.

I walked past row after row of cages. One beagle per cage, all happy to see me, tails wagging. They rushed to the front of their cages, hoping I would pet them or to perhaps receive an unscheduled meal. The dogs in our initial study had their own row of cages. Since we didn't know how much protection our liposome compounds would provide (if any), we had to start with defining a basic dose curve, similar to an LD_{50}. That meant some dogs would receive very high doses of indomethacin, while others received none. The rest received various dose levels in between. The first study lasted a week.

On the last day of the study, a technician brought the animals one by one to a cold steel bench-top. The dogs were so happy to be held and clearly enjoyed the attention immensely. While they were supposed to be taken out and played with each day, that activity certainly lasted no more than a few minutes, if it was even done at all. Most facilities are self-regulating in those matters, with no federal oversight. In the arms of a technician, tail wagging and face licking was the first dog's primary concern as the on-staff veterinarian injected a lethal dose of barbiturates into a vein in the dog's forelimb. What was once a bundle of joy and happiness quickly and silently sank into a limp and lifeless form. The eyes, once lively and seeking, were now silvery blank and no longer had the intense and indescribable depth of the living. My own reaction was surprising even to me—I could only watch this procedure one time. It was simply too much. Instead, I returned to the bench they had set up for me and waited for my tissue samples. My only solace was that the suffering agony I had witnessed in the severely traumatized high-dose dogs would soon be over. This was much different than rats, somehow. I was quite sobered by the whole thing.

When I was about twelve, living in Illinois, my parents had a giant purebred St. Bernard named, appropriately enough, "Edelweiss." They bought her as a puppy to entertain their fantasy of competing in dog shows. She was a majestic and beautiful creature, full of love and exuberance for our attention. It was attention she craved more than anything else because such a large and slobbery dog was more than my parents could really handle. Both of them had full-time careers as well as two young children, and the level of training and discipline that was required to show a behemoth such as Edelweiss was far in excess of what they possessed. In her first home as our new puppy, she had the run of the entire back yard, as it was fully fenced. As an adult in our new home, however, she was kept in a relatively small outdoor run that always seemed to be muddy and stunk immensely with her enormous piles of feces. She rarely had any interaction with the family apart from feeding time, and no other dogs kept her company. On exceptionally cold nights, my dad brought her into the basement where she was tied to a post to prevent her from getting into the lab or into any of the other valuable treasures my dad stored within reach. Only upon looking back now do I see how horribly sad and neglectful her living conditions were. At the time, though, it was just the way things were.

The aspect of neglect really hit home and hit hard one day when my parents returned from the vet. I had never before seen my father cry and he was weeping and sobbing non-stop. I was completely dumbfounded and had no idea what was going on. Finally, my mother explained to me that Edelweiss had heartworm as a result of mosquito bites. She had so many worms that only open-heart surgery would be an option and even then, there was a very slim chance of her survival. I saw how crushed my father was and how he blamed himself mercilessly for their negligence. Edelweiss was subsequently put to sleep; she was taken away in our station wagon and never came back.

One by one, all fifteen experimental beagles were killed. "Euthanized" is the proper technical term, which serves to help distance the actual act of killing from any feelings that might arise in those people responsible for it. They were each taken to a necropsy room where unknown technicians removed their stomach and intestines for me to analyze (all part of the service the breeder provided). My procedure was the same as for rats, except that the samples were much larger. While an opened rat's stomach was the size of a quarter, the beagle's is closer to the size of a bread plate, roughly eight inches in diameter. Wet with saline, the healthy pink wrinkles contrasted strongly with the blackened regions where the stomach lining was gone and replaced with open bloody sores. The intestines were also correspondingly larger, although relatively shorter, as one would expect from a carnivore. Like the stomach lesions, the intestinal ulcers were also quite familiar to me, having looked at so many rats prior to this. Measuring the ulcers with calipers took much longer, however, and I spent several days processing all the samples from this study. By the time I flew back home with data to plug into our computers, I was certain that I was not going to enjoy processing more dog samples. I knew that hundreds of samples would soon be forthcoming, as new dog studies had already been started at this facility before I left.

Each week, new samples packed in ice arrived via FedEx from the beagle company and I spent a day or two measuring ulcers. In between the regular boxes of cold Ziploc bags filled with dog intestines and stomachs, I was still performing other studies with rodents. I was continually immersed in the death and misery of animals, but because it was clinical, relatively clean, and professional (science!) it all seemed normal and nothing to get concerned about. After all, this was what was needed to discover better treatments for disease.

Finally, the day came when I left the company. More accurately, I switched gears. My group's studies (as well as those of other groups) were not yielding as much success as originally hoped for and the company was losing financial backers. By this time, however, I had also become one of the company's primary computer gurus and was responsible for maintaining the dozen or so IBM ATs they had recently purchased. While the rest of my group (including my boss) was laid off, I was contracted as a computer consultant. Thus began my new career in personal computers, which would last for ten years and take me down some wonderful paths of what was then cutting-edge technology and give me the freedom of self-employment. The last thing I expected was to end up back in animal laboratories. It seemed, however, that my career as a vivisectionist would not be over just yet.

And the worst was yet to come.

CHAPTER EIGHT

A New Life, A New Death

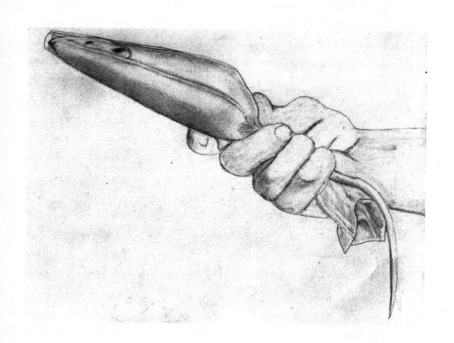

Connie didn't like ferrets. It was understandable; not everyone does. They have a distinctive musky odor that permeates their entire being, even if they have been surgically "de-scented." They are almost hardwired to be mischievous and have the non-stop habit of getting into everything, everywhere. Even when they are asleep, and thus presumably not getting into trouble, they are no doubt dreaming of causing a mess. Their main occupation in life (along with cats) seems to be take anything that is above ground level, and knock it quickly down to ground level. If the object breaks in the process, that is not their concern. The fact that they do it with a smile on their face and playful hops as they run around ensures that they are forgiven within mere seconds after their evil deeds are committed.

Moving in with my girlfriend was easy enough. I didn't have too many possessions and even though the place was cramped, it was still comfortable. Except for Frank. Frank was not welcome in our tiny home and even though he was used to having my entire room to run around in, I was forced to build him a cage to live in—outside. I built a sleeping box inside of it, and the wire mesh floor in the rest of the cage assured that his waste would fall through. I didn't want to have to clean his cage too often and this seemed to be the most efficient design.

Everything seemed to be ok for a while. I visited him and played with him, taking him out for a romp in the yard whenever I could. I knew it wasn't the same as the freedom and social interaction that he had before, but what could I do? I placed his cage beside the front walk so that he was always greeted anytime I came and went.

My life was busy. A new relationship, a new home, work, my very first IBM PC clone. . . . I didn't have much time for Frank anymore. Winter came. One day, Frank didn't come out of his box. I reached inside to discover only cold fur covering his stiff body. I was absolutely crushed. I knew immediately that the cause of his death was through my own neglect. I hadn't been checking on him as often as I should have and now I'd killed him. No amount of consoling or rationalizing ("He was probably old anyway") from my girlfriend would soften the emotional damage that I felt over what I did to him. My sheer stupidity and lack of *empathy still haunts me today. Tragically, it wasn't the last time I would accidentally kill one of my beloved pets through stupidity or negligence. I never once reacted to the deaths of my research victims in this way.*

A new life.

While working at Applied Lipids, I became romantically involved with a co-worker in another research group, named Connie. This relationship distracted me from nearly everything else at the time.

When I helped her with her guinea pig studies, I didn't think twice about the pet guinea pigs my sister loved so much. I barely glanced in the rabbit room where other researchers were testing drugs on the eyeballs of rabbits. Rabbits lined up in rows of small boxes in which they were confined so that the animals couldn't rub their eyes. Some days, walking past that room, I would notice people removing the rabbit's eyeballs for study. The biohazard bags filled with the corpses of rabbits were always much larger and heavier than my mouse or rat bags and always took up too much space in the storage barrels where we deposited discarded tissues and dead animals. That was my primary annoyance with their rabbit studies, not the continual abuse of so many innocent beings. I was glad that I didn't have to work with them, however. Rabbits are so much larger and not as willing to be subjected to the horror of research as rats and mice. Furthermore, a good kick from their hind feet and sharp nails would easily shred skin, if not handled properly. But all of that was unimportant to me. I was going to get married!

In hindsight, the marriage was doomed to fail, as I got married for the wrong reasons. I guess I never have been very good at planning long-term goals for myself, and this was not any different. In the past, I usually dated anybody who showed the least amount of interest in me, whether or not they were really a good match, and I followed that same trend with Connie. My myopic perspective probably reflected my relatively low self-esteem and shyness when it came to dating. I almost never approached a girl. Instead, I would date whichever one approached me first. The good thing about this was that I was never rejected. The bad thing was that I was rarely happy with the relationship for long.

Connie and I actually had a lot in common though. Not only did we work in the same field, we were also both very interested in other sciences, had the same progressive political and non-religious ideologies, both loved books, and enjoyed much of the same taste in humor and music. She was six years older than me, but we shared most of the same pop culture references. The biggest difference was that she was born and raised in central New Jersey and had a lot of family nearby, while I had just arrived there during my teen years and only had my parents and sister. I enjoyed most of her family, however, and we all seemed to get along fairly well. Her mother made an incredible rum cake, assuming you didn't crack a tooth on a piece of walnut shell.

At the time we met, I was renting a room in a house not too far from work, the downstairs of which was being used by the home-owner as a graphic design company. It was a good arrangement. The people working there were in their late twenties like me, and had great attitudes and senses of humor (things I always value in others). It was conveniently located and the rent was affordable. However, it was not very close to where Connie lived and I was spending most of my free time at her place anyway. We decided it would be best if I moved in with her.

Her rental home was a really interesting little bungalow in an old suburb outside of Trenton, having once been used as a streetcar. At some point in the past, additions were built onto each end of the streetcar, so there was a kitchen on the north end and a tiny living room and an even tinier bedroom on the south end. The streetcar section connecting the two ends was really just a long window-lined hallway with a miniscule bathroom, only barely large enough for a shower, sink, and commode. Any empty wall space around or beneath the windows was used for our books. It was as cramped as it was unique.

Connie lived alone with a canary she adored who would fill the air with his singing every day. She hung his cage outside when the weather was nice and he seemed to enjoy that immensely. It wasn't long before I felt the need to add more pets, however. Through one of her brothers, I learned about a 250-gallon glass aquarium that was mine if I could haul it off. It had a small leak, which flooded the pet store where it was used as a display tank under the checkout counter. A cut on my wrist, a sore back, and a tube of caulk later, I had a gigantic six-foot-long aquarium in my possession. Somehow, I managed to shoehorn that tank into the streetcar, and I bought a caiman to live in it.

I really don't know why I decided at the time a caiman would be a good idea. They are small crocodiles, only reaching three to four feet long at their maximum, but I did not think that far ahead. The little guy I bought was only twelve inches long and, even though he was (and would always be) aggressive, I managed to keep my fingers away from his mouth. I bought "feeder" goldfish for him to eat and discretely bred mice at work so I would have an ample supply of "feeder" baby mice too. It was not allowed for anyone to keep pet rodents at Applied Lipids, but a couple of us did (for whatever reason) and it was tolerated as long as it didn't get out of hand. About this time I also brought home a feral kitten.

The place was packed. In addition to the ferret outside, we had a canary, a kitten, a baby crocodile, a retired show dog, another large aquarium with some piranhas, and two adult humans, all in a tiny one-bedroom home. It wasn't long before the crocodile reached two feet long and became unmanageable. I found a home for him, but once the aquarium was empty, I decided that a Chinese crocodile lizard would be a good pet to replace him with. It turns out that at the time of this writing, there are only about one thousand specimens still alive in the wild, the decline mostly due to habitat loss. I didn't know at the time that I would contribute to the species becoming endangered, or I wouldn't have bought him. The lizard lived about a year in my inept hands. Because neither of us understood cat behavior at all and were getting frustrated with her bouncing off the walls of the tiny space we lived in, we found a new home for the young cat too. When Frank the ferret died, I finally realized that I was not the good caretaker of animals that I had imagined. Of course, that didn't stop me from hoarding animals.

It was time for us to move into a bigger place. We settled on a two-bedroom garden apartment close to work. Connie hated leaving that streetcar, and I felt guilty for pulling her out of it, but we just got married and something had to give. Of course, we brought all the remaining animals with us and I had a couple turtles who now lived in the giant aquarium. The new place allowed me to have an office where I set up my new computer and it was about this time that my rather sudden and deep infatuation with personal computing blossomed.

I read everything about personal computers that I could get my hands on, subscribing to at least five different magazines. It was the late 1980s and the whole computer industry was experiencing explosive growth. New technology was coming out every month with exciting developments showcased on the turn of every page, and faster and better PCs were continually coming out at lower and lower prices. It's hard to describe the fervor that I and an entire generation of geeks were feeling as we were swept up into this brave new world of bits, bytes, and pixels. I had a couple of early personal computers before this (Commodore and Tandy), but they were either underpowered or not fully compatible. IBM was king and if you didn't have an IBM or an IBM clone, you were going to be left behind. Even early on, I knew I wasn't about to be swept up into the cult of Apple Computers—I preferred the generic world of do-it-yourself computing, not handholding by a single company. My mother, a teacher, was thrilled by all the new technology Apple donated to hundreds of schools, including her own. She was 100% Apple and had been since some of their earliest models were released. I considered it drinking the Kool-Aide.

With the help of Ronald Reagan and the Culture of Credit that had also swept the nation at this time, I was able to spend a thousand dollars on the parts needed to build my own powerful IBM clone. It had a 286 microprocessor (the same as the IBM AT), a megabyte of RAM, and a whopping huge 40-megabyte hard drive! I was in heaven. My previous computer didn't even have a hard drive and I had to settle for doing everything on 360-kilobyte floppy discs. I had one floppy disc drive for the software I ran and the other to store that program's data. Now, however, I had a hard drive and the latest high-capacity floppy drive, a 1.2mb unit. I even had EGA graphics (sixteen colors at 640x480 resolution). Since Windows wasn't out yet, I didn't own a mouse and did everything in MS-DOS. I became pretty proficient in writing batch files and other amazing DOS programming maneuvers that have since become relegated to distant nerd history.

Connie wasn't impressed. She enjoyed reading and this obsession I had with computers was of no interest to her. Since I leveraged my new computer skills into my becoming Applied Lipids's computer tech, it made things a lot easier for me when I was laid off. I simply stayed on as their "computer guy." I was now their consultant and with the help of a couple connections, I managed to get a second local biotech startup as a client. Between the two of them, I was on my way to a life as a professional computer geek.

For the next several years I breathed, ate, slept, and lived for personal computers. I worked both as a consultant and as a bench tech for a little computer repair shop. I also began going to large computer flea markets that would come to the area fairly regularly. After talking to some of the vendors at these shows, I discovered something very exciting: a nearly nomadic lifestyle. Each weekend, dozens of small computer companies would go from town to town up and down the East Coast and sell their wares at these traveling computer flea markets. The tables were cheap to rent and I had a lot of leftover but functioning parts from the many upgrades my clients had me perform, so I figured I would just sell them at these shows. I loaded up my little car and headed out to weekly locations, everywhere from Boston to Washington, DC.

About this time, I was also becoming infatuated with "multimedia," which was at the time a remarkable addition of quality video and sound capabilities to what had previously been pure green text or low-level four-color graphics with only beeps, bleeps, and monotones for sound. I began to contact a few small companies that made low cost audio and video manipulation products and secured distribution rights to those items. This allowed me to not only sell these high-end toys to customers at the shows, but also to sell them to other vendors at wholesale. I was the only person at these shows with a video camera at my booth that allowed me to capture a customer's face in real-time and save it to a floppy disc for me to give them (the disc also had my product catalog on it). This always drew a good crowd and I was making pretty good money from it. I bought an early cellular phone (a five-pound "bag phone") that cost me one dollar per minute to use, but allowed me to call for verification on credit card purchases. I had a fancy banner, professional draping, and I printed twenty-page catalogs that I gave away at the shows. I even sent monthly bulk mailings of several thousand catalogs to addresses of potential customers that I purchased from mailing list brokers. Branching out into other products (the DVD-ROM was fairly new, for example), and making new arrangements with other small manufacturers, I was becoming a real deal-maker and even though I operated out of my home office, it felt great to be my own boss.

All of this travel (I was gone all weekend, every weekend—even holidays) and the business demands that took all my time during the week had its toll on my relationship. I constantly encouraged Connie to join me, and on occasion she would, but for the most part she had little interest in the whole affair. Then in 1990, trouble hit. George H. W. Bush invaded Iraq and began the first Gulf War. The world was suddenly transfixed to their TVs as CNN broadcast twenty-four-hour news coverage of every missile attack and bombing. The US headed into an economic recession and people were simply not spending as much money on the types of products I sold (which were, to be honest, just high-tech toys). I was transfixed by the war as well and I didn't move fast enough to readjust my business focus. I owed the IRS a lot of money and all my credit cards were maxed out. It was time to liquidate inventory and close shop.

The following few years were financially difficult. I worked several jobs both inside and outside of the computer industry, even selling phones at Sears where I had bought mine a few years prior. I finally ended up as the computer technician at a company that offered professional continuing education courses to accountants and lawyers. Even though Connie still worked as a vivisectionist, we were struggling to pay our bills, and I had never been very good at managing our finances. Meanwhile, my infatuation with computer hardware had finally given way to what was beginning to happen online and on TV.

One Saturday morning after watching *Pee Wee's Playhouse*, one of my many guilty pleasures, I happened to notice this strange show on Comedy Central. It was one of my favorite old B-grade science fiction movies. This time, however, the broadcast was different. There was a black silhouette of theater seats and three characters sitting at the bottom of the screen. They seemed to be watching the movie too. Intrigued, I waited to see what this was about. To my shock and wonderment, the characters were riffing on the movie, making wisecracks at everything that was said and done on the screen. Not just wisecracks, but *hilarious* wisecracks! I sat mesmerized through the rest of the movie. The characters eventually revealed themselves to be a sleepy-eyed human and two plastic puppets made to look like quirky robots, who were stranded in space and forced to watch cheesy movies by a mad scientist and his sidekick. I was immediately hooked and upon learning the name of the show (*Mystery Science Theater 3000*, aka, "MST3K"), I logged onto my computer to see if there were many other fans of this incredible gem of hilarity. What I discovered wasn't just a fan base of a hundred people, but instead something that would dominate much of my social life for the next ten years and still remains part of my life today (I even have an MST3K tattoo).

The Internet landscape at the time was vastly different than it is now. There was no World Wide Web outside of universities, and everything that was online had to be accessed through very slow dial-up modems. We had Internet Relay Chat (IRC) and newsgroups, but for any real social engagement, we had to either rely on small dial-up BBSs (bulletin board services) or subscribe to a major national service, such as CompuServe, GEnie, or AOL. Most of them were fairly expensive to use with any regularity and they charged by the minute. GEnie was much cheaper than the other two, but it was rather cumbersome to use and certainly no-frills in comparison to the others. When a joint venture between IBM and Sears announced their new service, called Prodigy, my ears perked up. It was graphics-based (albeit at a very low resolution), and didn't have live chat, but the most important thing was that they charged a dirt-cheap flat rate for unlimited use.

When I discovered the MSTies (as fans of MST3K call ourselves) on Prodigy, I truly found a new home and made dozens of what turned out to be lifelong friends. Before too long, AOL (which had awesome live chat) finally became affordable with a $19.99 per month flat rate. Because of this, most of us switched from the comparatively slow and clunky Prodigy to the slick Windows-based AOL to continue our cyber-friendships. We watched episodes of MST3K in live chat together, traded video tapes through the mail in order to collect entire seasons, got together in person at MST3K parties in cities across the US, and even appeared as fans in the television promotions run on Comedy Central. In a character costume, I introduced episode 420 during the 1992 Thanksgiving marathon, for example.

I know now that I nearly abandoned my wife in favor of the Internet and my new online friends. While I made every attempt to bring her into this great new world of MST3K and all the wonderful people I met, Connie wasn't interested. Eventually, I was spending every free minute online in my office, while Connie read romance novels in the living room. I even tried to get her interested in the online romance novel fan groups of Prodigy and AOL, but she didn't find that or anything else about the early Internet interesting either.

The marriage was doomed. Of course, there was more to our breakup than just AOL. We had been drifting apart in many other ways prior to this and the strain of our near financial ruin was a powerful force that wedged itself between us. Finally, our emotional separation was too much for me to sustain and I decided it was time to end the relationship. I realize there are two sides to every breakup, but looking back, I know I deserve much of the blame. I just couldn't understand why she couldn't be as fanatical about this show and its fans as I was, or at least why she wasn't interested in what was available on AOL and elsewhere online. I was truly dumbfounded, but I wasn't going to let her be my stick in the mud. Six years after getting married, I moved back in with my parents.

Since my parents were not willing to have their adult son live in their home again for very long, I was forced to find a new place quickly. Since my whole life outside of work was tied up in the social lives of my online friends, I soon found myself attracted to one of the young MSTie women I met on AOL. After countless hours chatting together online and after consulting with other MSTies who had met her in person and thus learning that she wasn't an ax-murderer (I found out later that she had done the same research on me), we decided we needed to have an in-person date. Lisa lived in Florida and I lived in New Jersey, so we met half way in Myrtle Beach, South Carolina, getting to know each other better over a weekend. It took all the strength I had to return to New Jersey when it was time to leave. After being sure that it was what each of us wanted, we decided to share a place together in Florida. That was 1993. We got married at midnight on December 31, 1999 and now, more than twenty years after our first date, we are still together.

However, our life together was rocky at first. We were dirt-poor, working as banquet servers at a country club while taking night courses when we could at the local community college. My former computer experience eventually landed me a good production planning job at Lockheed Martin. Yes, I went from doing industrial animal torture to making industrial war machines. Only looking back now do I see the irony of that.

I probably would have done fairly well professionally had I stayed there, but before long the time was right for us to find something better for Lisa, so she enrolled in an Engineering program at a state university, over a hundred miles away. Since her career prospects were much stronger with that degree than mine were with no degree, we figured that I could also try to work on my degree there and then find something better later. Since I had been mostly outside of the computer industry for the previous five years (an eternity by tech standards in the mid-late 1990s) and after struggling to find anything that paid close to what I was making at Lockheed Martin, all I found in the college town was more animal research.

CHAPTER NINE

A New Dungeon

The room smelled horrible! Something was clearly wrong, and it wasn't the ammonia smell of neglect that I had grown used to. I could always tell when the animal facility staff didn't change the cage bedding as often as they should, especially over the weekend. No, this was worse. Going over to the rack holding the shoebox cages with my mice, I immediately saw what was wrong. In one cage, the rubber stopper holding the sipper tube in the water bottle had been incorrectly seated, causing the entire contents of the bottle to flood the cage over the weekend. Four of my mice were huddled in the corner of their prison, soaking wet and shivering. All of them trying simultaneously and unsuccessfully to stand on the corpse of a fifth mouse in order to stay out of the stinking wetness. They would have to be destroyed, as their study was compromised. Looking at the rest of my cages, I noticed two more that were without any food. How long they had no food was anyone's guess, since it was a Tuesday after a holiday weekend. I sighed, knowing there was nothing I could do. Telling the animal facility supervisor was pointless. She would give me the usual platitudes about how they would make sure it didn't happen again, yet it happened all the time. Like anywhere else, when you pay people minimum wage, you often get minimum quality. And mice were a minimum concern in that dungeon.

This school was one of the large universities in Florida and I was thrilled to be there. It had perfect climate, natural beauty, plenty of nearby wildlife, and a top-tier football team. What more could I ask for? I was still very interested in the life sciences and knew that my experience in the lab was strong, so getting a job at their School of Pharmacy seemed the natural thing to do. Once again, I was going to do real science and this job paid almost as much as the Lockheed job. Free tuition was also a big bonus.

I have always loved college towns and working on campus was ideal for me. It was simply the perfect environment to satisfy my love of learning and all things academic. The Florida weather allowed me to ride my bike year-round the few miles to work, along scenic bike paths and through quiet neighborhoods. A bus stop next to our apartment allowed me free transportation on the days when weather was inclement.

The university's health science center was a large complex attached to the university hospital and my new lab was on the fourth floor in one of the three large buildings where research was done. A fairly busy lab, it was also much smaller than what I was used to at Applied Lipids, but at least the bosses were in another building on the other side of the research complex. A large terraced courtyard separated the buildings, which was where I spent a lot of time smoking cigarettes and joking around with my coworkers.

I should have known from the interview, however, that this was going to be a somewhat seedy operation.

My interviewer, who would become my direct supervisor, had her own large room in the other building across the courtyard. Her office/lab was poorly lit, dirty, and cluttered, looking like it hadn't been cleaned in years. I soon found out that that was indeed the case. Tall stacks of dusty papers and journal articles spilled off of every surface surrounding her desk, almost cocooning her chair and computer screen. Nested rat and mouse cages, the same type of shoe box-sized cages I used at Applied Lipids, were arranged in tall sloppy columns around the room, three- to four-feet-high. There must have been thirty cages, all of them vacant, except for their dirty bedding material and stale water bottles. Pellets of rodent chow were scattered all over the filthy floor. Bench space was cluttered with discarded syringes, needles, and vials of various poorly labeled liquids and powders. A mountain of sample tubes in their Styrofoam trays was propped up in one corner. Where I was actually able to see open surface area peeking out from all the dirty clutter, it was covered with torn and dirty bench paper heavily marked in numerous stains of different colors, the predominant stains appearing to be those of dried urine and blood. My hunch about that was also correct.

And the room had an odor. Not strong, but unmistakable. The smell was that of rot—very similar to what the animal disposal barrels were like at Applied Lipids, after they had been there for too long awaiting their pickup date. She apologized for the smell, claiming that a mouse had escaped a few weeks prior and she was unable to catch it. I nodded and smiled, although I was fairly certain I saw a neglected dead mouse inside one of the nested cages as I came in. A dozen trays of sample vials, filled with what looked like animal tissue, were also sitting nearby. I wasn't convinced that they weren't also an additional source of that faint, foul odor.

Despite the condition of her lab (something that would later become the butt of many jokes), the interview went well. She had a good sense of humor and her casual attitude did a lot to relax me and make me feel at ease discussing my prior experience. Her flippant and sarcastically snide comments about the research group and the primary investigator in particular, gave me a lot of confidence that she was someone I could enjoy working for, despite the filth of her lab. Once I was given a tour of the clean and well-lit lab space that I would inhabit in the other building, I felt much better about it. I guess she felt good about the interview too because I was immediately given a broader tour than I would have expected, had I been somebody who didn't pass muster.

A few doors down the hall from her lab, chemists were buzzing about like so many nerdy flies. They were busy hunkering over the results of this assay or that electrophoresis, running from one air-sucking fume hood to another, checking the temperature of a rotary-evaporator bath, or pipetting liquids from one flask to another. Piles of chemistry journals covered the desktops and dirty glassware filled the sinks. It was almost like a scene from a movie, except movies never seem to capture the dirty grittiness comprised of countless little chemical accidents and now-dried minor spills that will be "cleaned up later" but never are. And the smell. Movies cannot convey the distinctive odor of a chemistry lab. I think all chemical labs smell the same: acrid, sour, tangy, putrid and sinister. So many mysteries are concocted in chemistry labs and each one seems more deadly than the last. I think this was one reason I preferred zoology to chemistry. An animal was tangible, solid, and understandable. It was just like me, with flesh and blood, brains, and eyes. Chemistry was a reaction between various powders, liquids, and gasses, often predictable but only described by a secret language of letters, numbers, and weird symbols. Chemistry was math and it smelled weird. I was glad to move on with the tour.

The animal facility was huge. I had no idea that it would be so large or that it would be so well hidden. There were several routes to get there, but the most common one involved crossing the open courtyard and walking through a hallway of the nursing school, past multiple half-inch-thick cross-sections of the human body, freeze-dried, preserved in plastic, and mounted on the walls. A left turn led me past a couple of large showcase cabinets displaying dozens of large jars containing conjoined-twin fetuses and other human infant deformations. Beyond that, next to a large walk-in cooler where human cadavers were stored on shelves reaching floor to ceiling, each one awaiting dissection in an anatomy class, was a freight elevator that always smelled of formaldehyde. This old beast was cranky and didn't always work as expected, so it was only ridden when absolutely required. Next to this was an unmarked metal door where a small set of stairs led to the basement. These stairs were normally used instead and a key was required to open the windowless door at the bottom. Descending these stairs, regardless of how many times I did it, always made me feel like I was heading into a secret realm in another universe. The contrast between what was upstairs and what lay downstairs was like night and day.

The stairway door opened into one end of a long hallway. The walls of the animal facility were painted in a dingy, yellowish, cream color. It was clear that they hadn't been painted in a while, much less washed. While not actually dirty, per se, the walls still gave me the impression of being old and grimy. The floor was simply concrete that had been sealed and painted gray. Double swinging doors to the right opened into a darkened surgical area that I would come to know quite well. On both sides and down the entire full length of the hallway were dozens of windowless doors leading into suites of rodent rooms. A couple of times down this hallway, I encountered other hallways intersecting, each one with their own collection of rodent rooms. Quickly losing my bearings, I imagined this maze of hallways and doors must have taken up the entire basement area of the two research buildings and the courtyard, combined. Turning the far corner, we eventually passed the cage washing equipment (a giant steaming monster that took up the entire room), food storage rooms, loading docks, offices, and more rodent rooms. Turning another corner (I was thoroughly lost at this point), we walked past seemingly countless and mostly unmarked steel doors, each of which opened to kennels. I could hear dogs barking and sheep braying as I walked past. For some reason, I never expected livestock to be down there. After all, the school of agriculture was in a completely different part of the university. The sound of dogs wasn't welcome to me though, after my work for Applied Lipids. I was obviously still thinking like a speciesist, where dogs were somehow more important than rats, mice, or sheep.

My selective empathy was no more apparent than when I peeked into another kennel after hearing the sound of cats meowing within. I have a profound soft spot in my heart for cats. This was something I acquired as an adult, having before always considered myself a "dog person." I think it was because after rescuing and providing a safe home for a couple of them, I learned what cat personalities were really like and began accepting them for who they were, unlike dogs, whose behavior you can easily bend to your will and train to your every whim. Dogs make obedient victims.

The cats in the kennels knew they didn't belong there. They all looked scared and extraordinarily unhappy. To me, the lab dogs just looked bored, but like the monkeys, cats also seemed to know that they were in a prison. And these cats were tortured in a way that even then, in the midst of my own logical vivisectionist mind-set, I would not have been able to tolerate.

In addition to other brain studies performed on them, many of these cats had their spinal cords surgically severed, causing paralysis from that point down. Spinal and brain injury research was not something I would have been able to perform on cats and I was disgusted at the thought of it then as much as now. I remember being thankful that I didn't work for that particular group of researchers. Looking back, however, I know that I might have been able to do that to dogs, and certainly to rodents, but never to cats. Cats were special somehow. This warped thinking is an example of speciesism at its finest. I'm still befuddled how I couldn't see the irony of it then.

Because I hadn't yet received the required vaccines and medical tests yet, I was not allowed into the monkey rooms. This was to both protect the colony from highly infectious and deadly diseases that I might carry (such as tuberculosis) and to protect me as well. I was in for quite a surprise when I finally saw what was in store for both the monkeys and me.

CHAPTER TEN

Parade of Pain

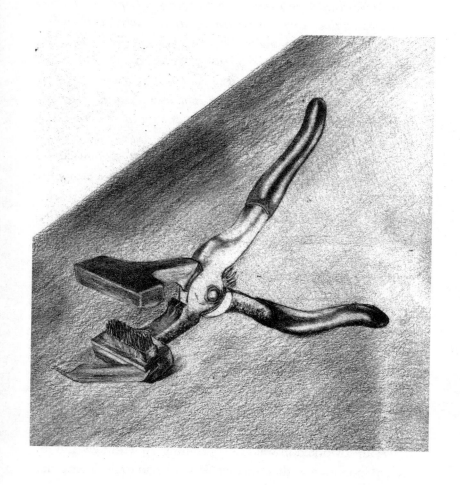

I shook a slender glass tube, about the diameter of a strand of spaghetti and four inches long, from the small plastic bottle. One end was printed with a red stripe, but that end was not important because it was too smooth. The interior of the tube was dusty—sodium heparin, to keep blood from clotting. I used a small metal saw blade with teeth too small to see to lightly score the tube in two places, dividing it roughly into thirds. Once I made the scores in the glass, the tube broke easily, giving me three new shorter tubes, but this time with relatively rough ends. You couldn't see the minute razor-sharp edges at these breaks, as the tubes broke cleanly, but I knew they were jagged. Taking a rat firmly in my left hand, fingers forcing his arms to cross, I looked at the bright pink eyes, naturally bulging out of their sockets. It was hard to tell what he was looking at. They were completely unlike the eyes of a cat or dog, which is probably why this task was so much easier for me to perform. Little droplets of a blood-red lubricant that they produce, porphryin, were on his nostrils, a sure sign that he was stressed. While holding his face over a heparin-coated sample tube, I twisted the sharp end of the glass tube into the inside corner of his eye socket. Blood immediately poured through the tube, filling up the vial. Sometimes they would jerk their heads, throwing the tube out of their eye, and I would have to stick another one in. Once enough blood was drained, I grabbed another rat and did the same thing to him. I was told this didn't blind them, but it was hard to know for sure; albino rats have very poor vision anyway. At some point I figured they must have gotten used to this ordeal, since I did it to them once a day.

I performed many different studies on many different rodents at the School of Pharmacy. None of them ever seemed to produce practical results because they were all based upon educated guesswork. Countless LD_{50} studies were an ongoing task for me, as the group I worked in was always coming up with new and untested compounds and their relative lethality had to be determined.

As always, mice were the typical species for this and injections and body counts were often the first thing I did each morning. Once a study ran its course, all the remaining mice who survived (often just hanging onto life by a thread) were sacrificed. More mice were then ordered for the next toxicity study in line, while five or six other studies ran concurrently. Cage after cage, mouse after mouse, body after body. It was just another assembly line. Occasionally, a facility staff member would mix up the cage tags when changing their bedding and the entire study had to be scrapped. All the animals were then killed. Occasionally, a water bottle would leak, flooding the cage and compromising those animals. Sometimes, food would be neglected or a lid would be left askew allowing escape. These types of things always meant that the animals were now useless and had to die. Other times, the wrong strain of mouse would be ordered by a coworker. Since it was unlikely to be a strain anyone else could use, those animals were also destroyed in toto. Occasionally, I made mistakes, injecting the wrong dose or hitting an organ or vein accidentally. More death. More replacement mice. All part of the cost of doing business.

While rats were the most common species used for my more elaborate studies and mice were the standard choice for the toxicity studies, occasionally mice would be needed for something else. In one study, for example, a compound was being tested that was supposed to affect the size of lymph nodes. I killed each experimental mouse and removed a popliteal lymph node from behind their knee and weighed it on an extremely sensitive balance. This lymph node is smaller than the head of a pin and locating and removing it with any consistency required me to practice on untreated mice. More dead mice. In the end, as with many other models, this study model proved unfeasible to execute and it was eventually scrapped.

In all of these kinds of studies, where tissues were harvested from mice or rats, I would take the animals back up to my nice clean lab and my nice clean lab bench where it was more comfortable for me to work. That usually involved stacking a bunch of cages onto a utility cart, covering them all with lab coats to prevent people from seeing them, and wheeling the whole thing through the nursing school hallways and across the public courtyard. In the lab, my radio would be blaring punk, funk, or grunge and my coworkers, mostly analytical chemists, would gripe and complain about both the music and the animals, frustrated by their futile inability to get me to refrain from bringing either into the shared space. I was in my element, doing work that I knew how to do well. Once my work was done, the dead animals were tossed back into an empty cage and the whole lot was wheeled to the basement—the cages went to the cage washing room and the bodies were dumped into a bag and taken to the incinerator room.

The incinerator room. This place was truly straight out of a horror movie. The heavy black steel door at the far end of a corridor, not far from the creaky (and most likely haunted) freight elevator, had a certain ominous quality to it. Not just because of what lay on the other side, but the fact that, unlike most other doors in the facility, there were numerous black scuffs and deep scrape marks on the floor leading up to the door. A lot of heavy objects were moved in and out of this room regularly.

No matter how many times I had to go in there, once inside, I always immediately wished I were someplace else. The smell was what hit you first. It was the dry, toasty, sickening smell of burnt hair. The room was always poorly lit, almost by design. A couple of dusty light bulbs were suspended from a dark, high ceiling in wire-protected cages. To the right were a couple of large chest freezers and to the back and left was the incinerator itself.

On the floor immediately to the left of the door, sat a lidded rectangular box made of steel, about the size and shape of an old-fashioned storage chest. Next to that box were a couple of four-foot gas cylinders, with attached plastic tubing running into the box. Dark (and clearly tasteless) humor was employed by some of the technicians who used that box. It was commonly referred to as "mauschwitz," and would hold several cages of mice or rats at a time, while the flow of carbon dioxide gas from the cylinders was turned on. A kitchen timer was sitting on a shelf so that we could ensure that enough time had passed, but I don't know that anybody used it. Most of the time, I would turn on enough gas to flood the box, then leave the incinerator room to attend to other tasks (or have a cigarette), only returning later to clean it out. I was not the only person who did this. More often than not, I would open the box to kill my animals only to discover the corpses of a dozen or more animals left there by another technician and forgotten. I would grumble about there being nothing worse than cleaning up the mess left by others as I dumped the cold, stiff bodies into a bag and put them into one of the freezers. Usually, the freezers were full of animals already and I would have to shuffle them about to make room. Such inconveniences irritated me. Sometimes, they didn't employ enough gas before leaving and I would open the box to find some of them still alive—barely conscious, wet with urine, and panting. Not only would I have to destroy my own animals, I would have to kill theirs too.

The incinerator was a giant black box about ten feet high and five or six feet across. It dominated the room. A large solid chimney led from the top of the box up into the ceiling. At about chest height, a metal arm swung up and down to open a sliding door, allowing the addition or removal of animal remains. The animals were dumped in as cold dead corpses and shoveled out later as chalky white ash. I never operated the incinerator because that was the job of the facility staff, but curiosity led me to examine this device a little further.

Near the front of the unit were two metal trashcans that contained the ashes of animals who had been previously incinerated. I could see bone fragments in that dust and that had me intrigued. By this point in my life, I had become an avid skull collector, having added quite a few specimens to my original childhood collection. Perhaps there would be something I could collect from this place too. Opening the incinerator door, I was amazed. Sitting in plain sight, right in front of piles of ash and bone, was a perfectly intact, absolutely white, alligator skull. The fact that it was an alligator wasn't so surprising, as this was a university in Florida after all, and I knew they did research on them here. What surprised me was how perfect this skull looked. Every detail of the bone was intact, with not a blemish or discoloration anywhere. It was a true work of natural art. Tentatively, I reached in to remove it and to my dismay, the moment my fingers touched it, the skull collapsed into a pile of angular fragments and chalk. Without the proteins to bind the mineral elements of the bone together (they had burnt away), the skull had become as fragile as crystalline lace. This object of beauty was gone forever, as was my naive hope of ever retrieving any skulls from that device. I never once thought about the living being that was incinerated, however. He was just another dead gator and his skull was the only thing of interest at the time.

My longtime interest in skulls and bones had never really disappeared. If anything, it had grown. While I was currently employed in the field of biology, my irrational fear of math and my interest in the humanities found me studying along much different lines. I could only take one or two classes per semester, but I decided that it would still be worthwhile to pursue any degree, even if it wasn't biology or one that would help me find a good job. After all, the university gave me free tuition as part of my employment, so it would be foolish not to take advantage of it. Looking at my earlier transcripts from community colleges (and keenly aware that the subject was also highly interesting), I saw that the shortest path to a Bachelor's degree was Anthropology.

Anthropology studies in the US follow four different paths: cultural, physical (human evolution and skeletal anatomy), linguistics, and archeology. While I was required to study many elements from each discipline, I was drawn to archeology and physical anthropology the most. I was (and am) truly enthralled by the evolutionary biology of all species, and humans are just another animal from that perspective. Studying human bones was almost as fun as studying the bones of other species. Even though I wasn't all that interested in the pottery shards and stone tools that seemed to be the focus of a lot of archeology, that field also involved the study of bones—animal bones!

The subfield within archeology that studies animal bones is called zooarcheology. Unlike paleontology, which studies only animal remains, zooarcheology's goal is to determine how animals were used by humans in antiquity, based upon animal remains as found within an archeological context. Through excavation (often of ancient rubbish piles), it can be discovered which animals humans ate, how they were hunted and butchered, and even how they were prepared in meals. In addition, the animal remains tell us a lot about the climate during the time of occupation and even details of trade and human migration. Seasonal variations of available species at any given time can reveal what time of year a temporary campsite may have been built, for example, indicating a seasonal hunting pattern. The discovery of guinea pig bones at an inland site hundreds of miles away from the only island where that species is naturally found indicates potential trade with people from that distant island. Or, depending upon other artifacts, it may indicate seafaring behavior of a people who were previously considered to have never left their shores.

I was thrilled to be pursuing this field and made good friends with the curator of zooarcheological specimens at the university's museum. Not only did she teach me a lot about the field in general, but I also assisted in sorting and cataloging her bone specimens in my spare time and was constantly being quizzed by her to identify this bone or that bone as I went along. One time she gave me a large box of bones and asked me to sort it into the two distinct individual sheep contained within. It's not everybody who spends a weekend at home with two large animal skeletons neatly spread out over their entire living room floor, working on a giant macabre puzzle.

One of the requirements for being a successful zooarcheologist was having a reference collection of animal bones at your disposal to which you could compare specimens. I certainly had a head start on that! I don't know if it was the fact that I had already amassed a large number of skulls and bones throughout the years, but she must have eventually seen my strong enthusiasm for the subject because I was even asked to help edit a textbook that she was writing. It was, and still is, the only textbook on the subject. I considered that to be quite an honor and I looked forward to entering a graduate program under her, but as is often the case, life's path would eventually take me away from that dream. In the meantime, however, I was still working in the lab.

Hamsters were not used in research as much as I had always thought. Most laboratory animals are bred for an amazing amount of docility and trust. Rats and mice rarely bite unless they are provoked, and even old male rats who usually become more aggressive in time will allow you to handle them without any protective gloves. Non-abused lab mice and rats are curious and seemingly happy to get to know this giant ape dressed in white. This is not so much the case with hamsters.

When I was a child, I had pet rodents of every variety: rats, mice, gerbils, guinea pigs, rabbits, and hamsters. Unlike my sister who loved her pet teddy bear hamster more than anything, I really disliked the little monsters. They always bit me. Like most other rodents, they are nocturnal, which usually means that during the hours when kids want to play with their pets, these creatures are trying to sleep. All other rodents will wake up and tolerate the intrusion without any apparent qualms, but if you even lightly touch a hamster who is sleeping, he will turn like lighting and put two excruciating holes in your fingertip. At least, that was my experience growing up.

During the course of the hamster study that I was asked to perform, I learned that, like many humans, waking them up slowly is much more conducive to their being in a good mood. In fact, the hamsters I worked with in the lab turned out to be much more docile than the ones I had as a child. That made my task all the more difficult because they did pull on my heartstrings more than

I expected. Part of the reason for that was the brutality of the experiment itself, but I think it was also because of a glimmer of compassion that was starting to appear in the back of my mind.

Unlike rats, whose ear tissue is sturdy enough to be pierced with a metal identification clip, hamsters have ears nearly as thin as paper. Any attempt at clipping a numbered tag to them would eventually prove fruitless, as it would certainly tear through the silky, thin membrane. Instead, a system of identifying holes are punched into their ears. This is done without anesthesia. A small steel tool is used, similar in size and shape to little nail clippers. Instead of having a pair of cutting blades like clippers, however, this tool punches a tiny, perfectly round hole through their ear exactly like holes punched in paper, but only about the diameter of a pencil lead.

The quantity and positions of the holes, and whether they are in the right, left, or both ears, determined the animals' ID. For example, a group of hamsters in my study might have IDs such as 1R (one right), 1L, 2R, 2L, 1R1L, 2R1L, etc. It wasn't necessary for my study, but there are very elaborate numbering schemes often used when one is dealing with large quantities of animals. One method involves powers of ten being punched in one ear, while holes indicating zero to nine were punched in the other. This ear allows the researcher to effectively identify and number up to one hundred animals.

Obviously, this ear mutilation is painful to the hamsters and they would frequently squeal and try to bite. Occasionally, the punch wouldn't release quickly enough and it would tear through their ear as the animal violently pulls away. That meant new ID holes would be required in the other ear, or it would be given a different code (e.g., TR for "tear right"). I would also punch holes in mice ears on occasion, but because most of my studies involving mice usually dealt with aggregate data from larger numbers of animals (mice being small and cheap), they were not often identified as individuals and so were able to avoid this treatment.

Ear notching is also used on larger animals, such as pigs, for quick identification. You will often find something similar done to cats in capture-neuter-release programs, as a means to quickly identify a feral cat already neutered. When a marked cat is caught again, it's released right away. One cat my wife and I rescued a few years ago is missing the tip of her ear for this reason. At least that's done while the animal is under anesthesia and for a reason that benefits the animal.

Another form of identification involves tattooing the inside of rabbit ears (for example), using a multi-needle punch tool with changeable letters and numbers. At least I never had to do a far more barbaric form of identification: toe clipping. As you may have guessed, this practice involves different lengths of different toes being clipped off the feet of smaller rodents, such as mice, hamsters, and rats, as a means to identify individuals. The rationale behind this is to establish long-term identification, as ear punches will eventually heal closed on their own. This is also usually done without anesthesia. As revolting as that sounds, I know that if I had been asked to do that to my test subjects as part of my job, I would have done it without question, or at least with minimal hesitation. After all, I was already willing to stick broken glass tubes into their eyes.

The hamster model I used was designed to test for treatment of infection in their cheek pouch. The continually moist and wet conditions, combined with low amounts of saliva rinsing meant that an infectious agent could be easily established, and topical as well as systemic treatments could be studied. In order to create the infection in the pouch, a controlled injury was followed by inoculation of the injury with the infectious agent.

I took the hamsters from the animal facility back to my lab, where I knocked them out briefly with carbon dioxide. Similar to the ether I used at Applied Lipids, this was also risky to the hamster because using that gas also meant the window of unconsciousness between being fully awake and dead is exceedingly small. The benefit was that I didn't have to breathe the harmful and explosive fumes.

One at a time, I would take a limp hamster, insert a pair of toothed forceps into his mouth, grab the highly elastic cheek, and pull it outside of his mouth while turning it inside out. I then applied a tattoo punch tool, normally used on rabbit ears, to the raw cheek. This tool was like a pair of pliers, with a broad, flat, smooth surface on one jaw and a slot on the opposite side. Changeable letters, numbers, or symbols, comprised entirely of dozens of sharp needles, are fixed into a metal slug that slides into the slot on the pliers' jaw. When the jaws are closed together onto flesh, the needles pierce all the way through until they meet the smooth surface on the other jaw. Normally, ink is applied to the needles first in order to produce a permanent tattoo in the skin, but in this case, the goal was simply to cause consistent and repeatable tissue damage to the inside of the hamster's mouth.

After tucking the injured pouch back into his mouth, I next inoculated each of the study animals with an infectious agent by flushing their injured pouch with a solution containing the study organisms—either bacteria or fungus, depending on the compound being studied. Each of the control groups, who were also injured, received either saline alone (i.e., no inoculation) or were inoculated and not treated (worst case baseline). The rodent would often wake up very shortly after the procedure. No attempt to alleviate pain was ever used.

After several days were allotted for the infection to become established, I tested various treatments. More experimental compounds were tried, more tests. I killed dozens of animals, cutting their cheeks out of their faces and analyzing the level of infection. Nothing ever came of these studies, despite dozens of attempts to get the model to work. Again, failures such as this were considered a normal but unfortunate waste of time and resources. There was, however, very little thought given to the suffering and brutality involved.

Like several of the rats and mice I had rescued to be my pets, I also brought one of the hamsters home rather than kill him at the end of his study. As a pun referencing a popular cartoon from the

1960s, I named him "Dudley 2-Right" because he had two holes in his right ear. He lived out his full normal life span in a small lab cage in my apartment. Despite the torture I had put him through in the lab, he never once turned to bite me when I woke him and picked him up.

The failure of this model was not a big surprise to anyone. Most of our studies failed, regardless of the lab I worked in. Is that the case for all animal research, or was that only true about my studies in particular? The truth turned out to be far more fundamentally horrifying than I expected. Years later, I learned that the actual failure rate of animal models used in biomedical research is a whopping 92%. In no other field of endeavor, whether industrial, educational, or pure research, is a 92% failure rate even remotely acceptable. Only in the use of animal experimentation is this inconceivable level of non-performance ignored as the "price of doing research."

Frequently, the blame is placed upon experiment design, the animal's environment, technician error, or other external issues that completely ignore the real problem: laboratory animals are not humans. No matter what physiological systems, cells, organs, or biological pathways are examined, the differences between humans and other animals are far too great to allow for any realistic comparison of how pharmaceutical agents will work between them. Even within the same species, differences between various strains of mice and even between individuals of the same colony frequently create worthless results. If a researcher can't be confident about results between two different mice, it's no wonder that the discrepancy between mice and humans is so large. Even non-human primates, who are much closer to humans on the evolutionary path, exhibit fundamental differences that have thwarted, for example, twenty-five years of research on HIV vaccines and treatment. Likewise, we now know that thirty years of diabetes research based upon the rodent model is fundamentally flawed because of basic differences between the cells of our pancreas and theirs.

We even see evidence of this in our own homes, as we are cautioned not to allow our dogs or cats to eat chocolate. Just the other day, I observed a squirrel eat an entire large toadstool, one bite of which would have sent me to the emergency room had I followed suit. Innumerable other examples exist.

Of all the laboratory animal instruments I used, perhaps none were as blatantly cold and unambiguously ruthless as the guillotine. There were times when a large blood sample had to be retrieved from rats at a very precise time point and/or when anesthesia would interfere with the sample. Fortunately, I didn't have to use it very often. I was glad for that because it was messy and required a lot of clean up. It was also a much more devastatingly gruesome thing to do—even to my jaded mind.

The animal was inserted headfirst into a disposable "plastic restraint cone," which was basically the corner of a large, clear plastic bag with a breathing hole at the tip, allowing only the nose to protrude. Holding the tail and firmly closing the bag around the rear of the animal, the rat was effectively immobilized and completely stuffed into what looks exactly like a clear icing bag used for cake decorating. His head was then inserted between the opposing V-shaped blades of the guillotine. Pulling the handle down in one swift motion, the blades cut through both the plastic and the neck, allowing the head to be "cleanly" removed. This is also considered an acceptable form of euthanasia, but the large number of animals that I routinely killed as well as the expense of keeping the blades sharp meant that I never used it for that purpose. It was also much more hideous than simply tossing the creatures into a box or pail and shutting the lid, where I was able to completely avoid the sight of their gasping for oxygen.

While gassing unwanted mice en masse was typical for the larger studies, a very common method I used to euthanize small numbers of mice (and occasionally rats) was through the simple method of cervical dislocation. I used any instrument that was handy—a pair of scissors, forceps, or even a ballpoint pen. While allowing them to stand on a surface and holding their tail, I would place the instrument just behind their ears, against their skull. With one firm move, I would simultaneously pull the tail down towards me and push the head away. The crunch and pop of the neck bones would tell me that I was successful. Their residual nerve response would cause all their legs to violently kick and jump for fifteen or twenty seconds. Finally, as their bodies stopped twitching, their bladders emptied and their bowels released. Occasionally, as I was learning the procedure, too much force was applied and they were decapitated. This method of euthanasia is still considered humane, despite the fact that a similar execution method for humans (hanging) isn't.

Sometimes an elaborate method of killing the animals was chosen specifically because of how the samples were to be collected. In one study, it was important that there be as little residual blood remaining in the tissues as possible. Normally, when an animal is sacrificed, the heart stops pumping and all the organs fed by that blood retain most of whatever blood is still in them at that moment. Some organs normally contain a lot of blood, such as the liver and kidneys, while others contain much less. Through perfusion, blood is replaced by another fluid, in this case, saline.

I heavily anesthetized each rat with an injection of barbiturates. They were completely unconscious and laying on their backs as I literally pinned them through their feet in a shallow wax-filled tray that was mounted over the lab's sink. This was also not popular with the chemists who shared the lab, as we only had one sink. The faucet was left running while I cut open their living body using a pair of stainless steel dissecting scissors. Since the animal was not going to survive the procedure, nothing as delicate as a scalpel was needed for this. When I cut the ribs away from the chest, the living, beating heart was fully exposed. After making an incision in the left ventricle with a sharp scalpel, I inserted a cannula and directed it up through the heart into the ascending aorta. When this was clamped into place, I made a large incision in the right auricle of the heart, and thick red blood would slowly pump out of this hole.

Opening the flow on the saline bottle mounted above the sink and attached by a narrow tube to the cannula, a lot more blood began to flow out of the hole. Slowly and steadily, the pressure of the saline, combined with the rat's normal heartbeat, flushed the blood out of the rat. The liver and spleen were no longer a solid, deep maroon color; instead they each began slowly turning a patchy pale brown. The kidneys also went from red to pale brown, while the lungs, previously pink, became ghostly white. As the exiting blood itself became lighter and lighter in color, the heart stopped beating. Eventually nothing even pink flooded out of the rat's now-dead body, only clear saline.

It was not lost on me how similar this procedure was to the embalming process. I then harvested the organs and placed each into their appropriate sample tubes. The faucet washed all remaining traces of their life down into a dark black drain, while I waited for the sedative to knock out my next victim.

CHAPTER ELEVEN

More Guts, No Glory

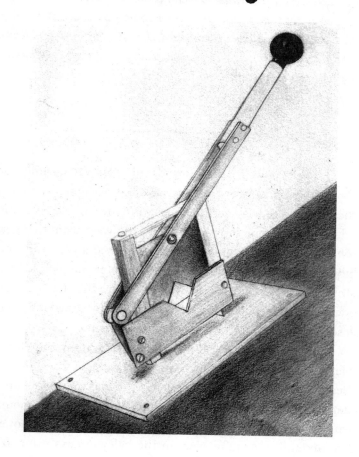

She was hired to assist with some of the rodent studies. Not having any real background with animal research, she needed to be shown basic procedures, such as IV injections in rats. This involves inserting a needle into the scaly and rather tough skin of the tail and finding the vein. It takes some practice and she was left with a few rats and a bottle of saline with which to practice. After returning a little while later to see how well she had picked up the procedure, I noticed that she was trying to hide something. It was obvious to me that she couldn't find the vein at all and had only injected saline into the tissues surrounding it, causing a lot of swelling. All the rats' tails had many wounds from multiple injection attempts, the needles no doubt becoming quite dull in the process. It was clear that she failed, but rather than get help or stop before any further damage was done, she denied that she had any problem at all and proudly proclaimed complete success. It should have been a clue right away that this technician wouldn't be helpful for our research, much less good for the animals.

———□——————————————————————□———

I don't know if it was considered when my resume was initially reviewed or if it was just my luck, but it seemed as though my earlier experience with rat intestines would follow me into this new job. For example, one series of studies I did was meant to determine if some of our drug compounds would work as an anti-diarrheal by inhibiting the secretion of fluids into the intestine. While I learned firsthand that there are many ways to induce diarrhea in a rat, this model was going to look more closely at the localized mechanics in one section of the intestine using cholera toxin.

Cholera causes death by severe dehydration and electrolyte depletion. An untreated human can expel three to five gallons of diarrhea per day. For our study, cholera toxin was therefore purchased under extremely controlled conditions. A very minute amount can poison large numbers of people and, for this reason, it is not a simple compound to acquire, even in the halcyon days prior to 9/11.

It was also incredibly hard to work with, requiring extraordinarily precise scales and careful formulation to achieve a dose dilute enough to use on something as small as a rat. Fortunately, I had chemists to do that for me.

Unlike most studies, each animal was its own control. I fasted them for twenty-four hours prior, and after they were fully anesthetized with barbiturates, I opened the rat's abdomen. Gingerly digging around in their belly with my fingers, I isolated a specific six inch section of small intestine. I tied off two segments within that section, each about two inches long, to prevent any passage of liquids between them. I then injected a tiny amount of the cholera toxin into each segment, followed by the test compound in only one of the segments. In order to prevent the tissues from drying out, I lightly closed the abdomen and covered it with saline-soaked gauze, while a heating pad beneath the animal kept their body temperature normal. After a specific amount of time had elapsed, I cut each segment from the animal and weighed them. The idea was that the untreated segment would weigh more than the treated segment, due to it having swelled with more fluid.

I did indeed observe incredible swelling of the control segment—it was a veritable water balloon. While one compound showed some minor success with this model, it was eventually deemed to be unworkable on a larger scale. There were several reasons for this: the inability to precisely control for the amount of toxin, the time consuming and elaborate nature of the surgical procedure, and the small number of samples that could be reasonably expected to produce data and therefore be statistically relevant. I was relieved. Not only was this study a pain in the neck to perform, but I also didn't like the thought of accidentally getting cholera poisoning from a tiny needle prick and having to spend several days in the hospital. At least the rats never woke up from this experiment and never had to deal with that kind of suffering.

While that animal study wasn't performed many times, another one involving diarrhea produced quite a bit more data, but to be honest, I don't know that I liked it much better. For one thing, the smell reminded me much more of the work I had previously done at Applied Lipids. I just couldn't seem to escape shit.

An age-old method of treating constipation is to swallow castor oil, a relatively safe product of the otherwise toxic castor bean. Its mode of action is still not understood, but it was the antagonist of choice for the design of this study.

For each of these experiments, I fasted twenty rats overnight in hanging wire cages. Each cage was like a wide drawer that pulled out from the rack. The drawer cages would often stick, so I had to shake and tug at each one to open them, often with a sudden jerk that terrified the rat inside. For this experiment, there was only one rat housed per cage. As I mentioned before, rats are gregarious; they do not like to be alone and they certainly don't like being in suspended cages, so they were emotionally stressed before the study even began. Five rats were used as untreated controls and, at each of three dose levels, I gave five others an experimental compound. I administered these doses either as a sub-cutaneous injection or via oral gavage. Thirty minutes later, I force-fed all of the animals with castor oil, purchased from a local drugstore. I took away their water and placed disposable aluminum trays under their wire cages.

As with many materials used in novel experiment designs, these trays were acquired through non-laboratory sources. They were collected after the whole department was treated to a bonanza of free of sticky buns, purchased specifically so I would have the trays that the buns came in to use for these experiments.

The study underway, I waited. I had a chair, my notebook, and a timer. As this was many years before smart phones were the distraction of choice, I also kept a paperback or a book of crossword puzzles with me. This was going to be a long, smelly day.

Looking back to my first interaction with laboratory animals at Applied Lipids, I recalled how I used to sit in the dark with a room full of rats. They would normally get twelve hours of light and twelve hours of darkness, but I would occasionally have injection time points that were scheduled during the dark cycle of their rooms. When you first entered a darkened room full of rats or mice, you would hear a cacophony of noise, as they were all running around, chasing each other, wrestling, eating, and generally doing what little rodents do for fun. The second you turn on the lights, they freeze. After a few more moments in the light, they would creep back to the furthest corner of their cage and huddle together. Often, the younger animals and those not yet experimented on would continue to play or sniff at the tops of their cages instead of cowering, curious to smell who or what might have entered the room (their albino eyes being mostly useless).

Sometimes I would enter the room while it was dark and leave the lights off. I would just sit on a stool for a few minutes and listen to them quickly resume their rambunctious play. It was absolutely exhilarating. I marveled at the multitude of rustling, squeaking, and running-about sounds made by the hundreds of animals. The sound would truly fill my ears and it honestly made me smile to think about how much fun was going on at that moment. Then, before I knew it, reality would set in. I was there to do a job and I had better get to it. I turned on the lights and I began to load some syringes.

Those were simpler times, I thought to myself as I listened to the occasional greasy drop of poop hit a tray. I spent a lot of time daydreaming while sitting in this new and different room full of smelly rats. How did I end up doing intestine studies again, ten years later and hundreds of miles away?

Every thirty minutes, I had to check each tray for the onset of diarrhea. It usually began between thirty and ninety minutes after the castor oil was given. I dutifully recorded this event in my notebook. I sat in the silence of that stinking room over the course of six hours, during which time the animals received no food or water. Every two hours I got up to weigh each rat as well as their trays, in order to measure stool output, recording each number in neat columns to be statistically processed later. Occasionally, a rat would uncontrollably release his bowel in the scale while I was weighing him, or on the floor as I moved him to and from his cage and the scale. I was forced to scoop up all the disgusting, goopy mess and place it into his tray so it could be measured correctly.

At the end of each study, I rinsed off the slimy, smelly feces from each tray, which I then neatly stacked on the bench to dry in anticipation of doing it all over again in a couple days. I usually killed all the rats at this point, although on occasion I would return them to their normal cages to observe if there were any fatal side effects from the drugs or if their organs needed to be harvested for analysis later.

Ironically, force-fed castor oil was often used as a torture method during Mussolini's regime in World War II Italy and by the fascist dictator Francisco Franco during the Spanish Civil War. As a form of punishment, force-fed castor oil was also often depicted in violent cartoons such as *Tom and Jerry*.

All during this time, my wife Lisa was a full-time student, working on her degree in Chemical Engineering. Therefore, her intense and total focus on solving mathematical equations each evening took all of her time and attention, especially since most of those equations appeared to be three feet long and (at least in my mind) the most confusing things ever created. I never really asked her what she thought about my work; she had so many distractions of her own at the time. It wasn't until several years after I left the lab that I learned how she felt about my work, when a friend asked her about it.

"Did you like the work he did?" the friend asked. We were driving to the store to get some food for a holiday party and I was absorbed in music.

"It didn't really bother me. I mean, it was his job. I personally never could have done it, though."

"Because you're opposed to it?"

"No, it's not that. His research advanced science and human health, so I'm not against it. It's how we get new drugs and cures," Lisa answered.

"Then why couldn't you have done it?"

"I don't think I could ever do anything like that to an animal. I'm too squeamish."

"But you didn't mind that Michael did it?" This friend had the habit of talking as though I wasn't there.

"It's a dirty job, but somebody has to do it," she laughed. "I know he didn't get any pleasure from it. It's just not for me. Just like I could never work in a slaughterhouse, but I like to eat meat."

I wasn't surprised by her answers. It echoed what most people felt about animal research. The fact that our friend was so curious about it was kind of annoying, however. I usually gave the same rationale whenever anyone asked me about it, but this friend was a vegetarian. I suspected ulterior motives beyond casual curiosity, but she didn't pursue it further.

As far as I was concerned, my life in the lab was old history and I didn't bring it up very often. Not because I was ashamed of it, but because it really didn't have any bearing on my day-to-day life anymore. Like everyone else, I benefited from prescription and non-prescription medication on a regular basis and even though my experiments never led to any great discoveries or wildly profitable or important cures, I knew that it was not wasted effort. At least, that's what I believed at the time.

Another gastric study I performed seemed to show some promise, and it was simultaneously more interesting and more boring than I expected. For once, the rats were apparently not going to be subjected to any physical pain and suffering. Just a little psychological torment.

Irritable Bowel Syndrome (IBS) afflicts an estimated 15–20% of people in the United States and several of the drug compounds we tested already showed results involving bowel motility. Both humans and other animals release their bowels during times of physical and psychological stress. Some rat experiments by other researchers have demonstrated the bowel-stress response through methods such as total or partial body restraint in cold conditions, or reintroducing them to a cage where they had previously experienced inescapable electric shocks. We chose to use another model that was used to demonstrate this response: the rat's natural aversion to water. While rats are willing to swim in order to reach a desired goal, they normally do not like to get wet and will avoid immersion if possible.

I took empty plastic rat cages and using vacuum grease, affixed a two-inch-high inverted glass dish to the bottom of each, as close to the center as possible. This created a nearly invisible island when water was added, up to a level very near the top of the dish. I lined up twenty cages on the workbench and filled each with water. Since rat rooms are kept a bit warmer than the normal room temperature comfortable for humans, it became humid rather quickly. Again, I came equipped with a chair, a timer, and a book. At least the smell would not be an issue with this study.

I injected rats with either the experimental drugs or a saline placebo and after thirty minutes, I introduced them to the water, one animal per flooded cage. While their feet were able to touch the bottom, they nevertheless quickly sought a way out of the water, eventually finding and climbing upon the small glass island. Presumably, its near-invisibility also invoked a stress factor. The rats would immediately begin drying and grooming themselves. Then I waited. And waited. Finally, after exactly thirty minutes, I took a pet store aquarium net and fished out each fecal pellet from each cage, carefully entering in my notebook the total number of turds I gathered from each animal. Then I sat down and waited again. This count was repeated every thirty minutes for six straight hours. When the study was over, I cleaned up the room for the next day's session. I got a lot of reading done.

While this study showed effectiveness of several compounds at low doses, in no way were these drug formulations non-toxic. In the toxicity studies I performed on mice, many of these drugs caused a whole gamut of neurotoxic symptoms. In addition to central nervous system depression and respiratory failure, the mice also displayed uncoordinated movements, tremors, and other examples of severe motor dysfunction, especially in the hind legs. These trembling and unsteady mice could barely walk. A few rats had to be removed from the water study after only a few hours because of similar neurotoxic reactions; they died within twenty-four hours from the drug's effects. After a few days following each study, the surviving IBS rats were also sacrificed, even the untreated controls. More rats were always available.

While a "wet rat" study was probably the least brutal in terms of animal cruelty, a model studying ulcerative colitis would be quite vicious in comparison. In a study designed to test for potential treatments for Inflammatory Bowel Disease (IBD) a rat model was chosen for relatively quick drug screening. The methods of this model were not only horrifying, but would take me completely back to my work at Applied Lipids.

I deeply anesthetized male rats with barbiturates and made an incision in their abdomen. I pulled their cecum (a large section of their intestine analogous to our atrophied appendix) and colon to the outside of their body. Just where the colon meets the cecum, I tied it off and then thoroughly rinsed the colon by inserting a syringe into the anus and flushing with ten milliliters of saline. I then squeezed any remaining saline and colon contents back out of the anus. Finally, I inserted a gum-based rectal plug into the anus.

One might wonder where a person could purchase such rectal plugs for rats. A quick glance through any laboratory animal supply catalog will yield a bewilderingly large and highly specialized number of devises and supplies for animal restraint and torture, but in some cases, a study's requirement is so bizarre that improvisation is required. The gum-based rectal plug was purchased from a local retailer. A convenience store to be exact. It was Wrigley's Extra chewing gum.

At this point, I used a needle and syringe to inject the experimental drug (or water placebo) into the colon, just below the ligature I made to tie it off. I then returned all of the intestines back into the body where they remained for thirty minutes. After that time, I pulled them back out, removed the anal plug, and squeezed the drug out of the rectum. Next, I slowly injected two milliliters of 4% acetic acid into the colon near the ligature, over a period of about fifteen seconds. Once an additional forty-five minutes had passed, I injected ten milliliters of air into the colon at the same place to blow out the acid. Finally, I removed the ligature, returned the intestines to the body, and closed the abdominal incision, using six to eight surgical staples.

I then returned the rats to their cages and allowed them to "recover" overnight. Twenty-four hours later, I killed them and removed their colons for study.

In cutting open the length of colon and spreading it out for photography and analysis, I experienced the more gory aspects of my biotech company job all over again. The acetic acid caused incredibly severe damage to their colons. In technical terms, it "elicited diffuse hemorrhagic necrosis." Whatever technical terms it was couched in, the pain and suffering these rats endured after awakening must have been intense. I have no doubt that they almost welcomed their deaths.

Fortunately, I didn't have to do this experiment very often, as it was being developed near the end of my tenure with the School of Pharmacy. In reviewing the published results, I later learned that this model showed some promise for some test compounds, but it was acknowledged that the acetic acid rodent model is not the best way to actually determine how well these drugs work in real IBD conditions, given the abnormally high acidic conditions of the colon in this model.

The irony of that seems to have been lost.

CHAPTER TWELVE

Flying Monkeys

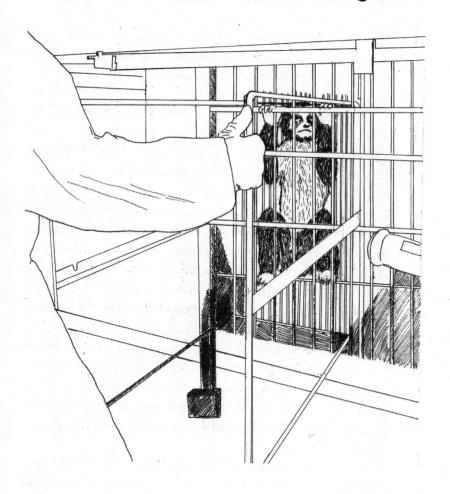

The little monkey cautiously looked up at me, meeting my eyes from his meek, downcast face. I could feel the gentle warmth of his petite brown hand through my latex glove as he held onto me for dear life. Tiny fingers and fingernails, much like a newborn infant, grasped onto my index finger as if asking for just a moment of love, just a little attention from his bigger cousin who seemed to control the entirety of the universe. Glancing nervously around as the other monkeys crashed and banged out their insistence that food be delivered immediately, he showed no interest in any of the treats I offered. His attention was fixed on my finger and my eyes. He maintained as much contact with me as possible, pressing his little body up against the bars of the cage in hopes that I would stroke him and never leave his side. This little monkey and his frightened little face was the beginning of the end of my career as a monster.

All of the rodent studies I performed at the School of Pharmacy were, for the most part, considered either basic toxicology or exploratory studies. None of them were really long-term, on-going, or in-depth research into the main work of our research group. Most of the monkey studies, on the other hand, certainly were. In addition to working with various rodents, I was also hired to work with Cebus monkeys, commonly called "organ-grinder monkeys" or capuchins. This is the species that is seen in countless television shows and movies, frequently wearing little red bell-hop costumes or other such "cute" ensembles in order to give them comical human characteristics. They are also kept as pets as well as service animals for the mobility impaired. Like nearly all the rodents I worked on, all the monkeys in our studies were male. Males were chosen for several reasons (including lower cost and minimal hormone fluctuation), but I found out later that their being male also complicated things.

Cebus is the genus name, but there are several different species, each with different body sizes and facial shapes, as well as differing fur styles and colors. There are some with white faces and shoulders, wearing a black cap, and with dark brown or black fur, while others are completely reddish-brown with long fur around their faces. While I worked with a mixture of different species, the most frequent one used was *Cebus apella*. Most of these individuals had short, light-colored hair on their faces, which were framed by darker fur around the sides and dark hair sticking straight up on top of their heads. The severe coloration of the more mature monkeys, especially on top of their heads, always made me think of Sargent Carter, the short-tempered and always-grouchy drill sergeant from the television show *Gomer Pyle*. I quickly found out that this same temperament also accompanied the looks. Heightened aggression in male primates is no myth.

Many of the monkeys who were there prior to my arrival had large ID numbers tattooed across their entire chest. However, new monkeys who came in since then had RFID chips injected under the skin instead. The tattoos made me think of prisoners in Nazi concentration camps, and despite the very tasteless nickname given to the gas chamber used to euthanize rodents, the full significance of the tattoo comparison was lost on me at the time.

My first introduction to the monkey colony was rather scary. There was no window in the door, so I didn't really know what to expect until I was already inside. The suddenly loud, cacophonous noise nearly made me jump out of my skin. The screeching, the crashing of metal on metal, the slamming of toys, the rattling of doors and food hoppers—dozens of monkeys jumping around wildly in their little metal boxes, frantically trying to get attention and to make it angrily known that they had something to say. It was almost nightmarish.

As a young four-year-old child living in Taiwan, I saw *The Wizard of Oz* for the first time in a local theater, within days of having also visited a zoo. Still to this day, one of my most vivid and creepy early memories is of the nightmare I had that night: I stood up in a crib and the entire wall on the other side of the room was filled with a giant troop of malevolent, scary flying monkeys, swinging from the trees and jumping or flying about in a very threatening manner, all the while looking directly at me. There may or may not have been glass between me and the monkeys (I don't recall), but above all else, I remember being absolutely terrified.

I think my coworker giving me the tour saw me noticeably cringe when we first went into the room, because she looked at me and laughed.

Once I realized that it was just noise and I wasn't going to be attacked, I was better able to examine the room I was in. After the noise, the next thing I noticed was the humidity. The temperature (78 degrees F) and relative humidity (60%) was set to replicate those conditions found in the monkeys' native environments—Central and South America. The place wasn't exactly a steam bath, but it was certainly more humid than most people like—and this was from someone who had grown accustomed to living in Florida over the past five years. The third thing I noticed was the smell. It was unlike any other odor I ever experienced, and having lived in Taiwan and Liberia, I had already been introduced to a bouquet of unique odors. It had an almost sour, tangy muskiness to it. Slightly fruity and earthy at the same time. It wasn't entirely unpleasant, but it was certainly unmistakable.

Like many of the other doors in the animal facility, the doors to primate colonies were always kept locked. This was to protect the monkeys from unauthorized staff members (and curious visitors) because they are highly susceptible to many human diseases, most importantly tuberculosis. Wearing a facemask, gloves, and a lab coat or scrubs was mandatory. Upon entering, and with the door closed and locked behind me, I found that I myself was now in a small cage. This tiny anteroom was made of strong steel wire mesh, mounted from floor to ceiling, and it completely enclosed me. Sturdy latches kept the door secure. Carefully closing the wire door behind me as I entered the main room, I remembered a similar double-door configuration I passed through when visiting an aviary at a butterfly park in Miami. The inner cage was meant to prevent an escaped monkey from getting out of the room! If one were to be free in the room while I walked through a normal single door system, he could rush past me into the hallway and become nearly impossible to ever catch again.

The room itself was not very large, considering the number of animals it housed and the noise they produced. It was probably less than fifteen feet wide and twenty-five feet long. Mounted along the entire length of both walls to the right and left were two continuous rows of steel cages, two rows high, for a total of about thirty-five cages. Each cage unit was about two-and-a-half feet wide, with a wire front, top, and bottom. The sides were solid. They were about three feet high and three feet deep. The waste fell through the wire bottoms of the cages, directly onto the floor from the bottom row units or onto a shelf that then drained back to the floor from the upper row units. A dirty coiled garden hose with a high-pressure spray nozzle hung on a hook at the back of the room. Large drains in the floor beneath the bottom row on each side were covered with sturdy iron sieves to prevent toys or other objects from falling through. Dog toys, shredded plastic water bottles, and "monkey biscuits" littered the floor. I don't know what sort of sterility I expected to find prior to entering the room, but it certainly wasn't anything close to the messy chaos I actually walked into.

A young woman was already in the room when I arrived. She was sitting on a chair with a clipboard, taking notes. Next to her was a tote bag full of hard rubber dog toys. I was told later that she was a psychology student and one of her projects was to study their behavior and to provide enrichment to these animals. I immediately wondered how anything could possibly be learned about normal behavior from jungle animals confined to tiny boxes. It turned out that she was the person who, in a well-intended attempt to provide enrichment, had polished steel mirrors installed on the walls in the room so they could see themselves and the others more easily. I was also told later that the addition of the mirrors seemed to increase the monkey's overall aggression quite a bit. They were later removed. We also regularly removed all of the plastic water bottles and rubber dog toys that she put into our monkey's cages in an attempt to relieve their boredom. The toys interfered with our ability to sedate the monkeys and our own tasks were always more important than the monkeys' sanity.

It turned out that I had reason to be somewhat afraid of these animals. Despite the fact that they are only about the size of a small house cat, a single bite could easily remove one's finger. They are extraordinarily strong, lightning fast, and because they are New World monkeys, they also have somewhat prehensile tails, meaning that they effectively have five limbs and hands with which to cause damage and destruction to person or property, instead of four. But here is the real underlying cause of their aggression and danger: we have taken (often literally) an animal straight from the jungles and forests, an animal that evolved to virtually fly through an environment of huge spaces and almost infinite treetops, and crammed them into a metal box no larger than the monkeys are long. Whether wild-caught or captive-bred, these monkeys have all gone truly insane after years of near-solitary confinement. I was definitely not dealing with cute pets or cheerful little movie stars in funny costumes.

Mostly because they were male, but also because we had to frequently remove them from their cages (no simple task), they were forced to live alone. These highly social creatures were unable to touch, much less groom another of their kind. They spent most of their days violently and noisily posturing with displays of aggression and dominance towards one another. When they weren't doing that, these highly intelligent animals were plucking themselves bald while rocking to and fro, or chewing up their toys in frustration and boredom. My supervisor never tried to downplay their warped mental state; in fact, she did quite the opposite. It was stressed upon me that because they had become so deranged over the years, they were incredibly more dangerous to work with.

But their eyes. . . . These were not the seemingly direction-less, virtually pupil-free pink globes bulging out of a mouse or rat face. These eyes were focused and full of expression. They showed fear, anger, curiosity, hunger, and desire. Their eyebrows arched with the appearance of surprise and frowned with concentration. Their mouths smiled, grimaced, and pouted. These animals showed more than a glimmer of sentience. In fact, they reflected a portrait of human. I tried not to think about that too much, but it was unavoidable.

They were forever trying to work the latches on the cage doors and trying to reach through the bars to their neighbor's cage. The cages were spaced far enough apart that their fingers could not meet, but occasionally it would happen. For this reason, a few monkeys were missing fingers. Other times, they managed to work their latch and escape into the room. This also led to injuries, not only because of contact with other monkeys through the bars, but because catching them required chasing them with a net. In their frantic desperation to avoid capture and through the typical animal facility technician's lack of skills, they would invariably get cuts, bruises, or even broken bones. While there was an on-staff veterinarian who regularly monitored their overall health and treated such injuries, escape was never a good thing for anyone involved, monkey or human.

Given their nature and the dangers involved, how did I extract them from their cages? It was a rather brutal process and always took two people. Within each cage there was another rear panel, the same height and width as the interior dimensions. Attached to the corners of that panel were long steel rods that extended towards the front of the cage and out the front. The top and bottom rods met together at the side of the cage, outside the front, forming a large "U" shape on each side. Normally this false panel remained pressed to the back of the cage, but when it became necessary to extract the monkey, one person would grab the two "U" handles and pull the entire rear panel towards the front. That person was usually me, because I am tall and able to do it while the other person ducks underneath. This squeezing took a lot of finesse and timing, because experienced animals knew what was happening and had developed effective tricks to prevent it from being pulled forward.

By wedging themselves with legs extended or through other body positions, the monkey's skill often meant it took several attempts to get it right. Typically, I had to shake the rear panel, quickly pushing and pulling it backwards and forwards until the monkey was in an optimal position. When the moment was right, I could then very quickly slam the press panel towards me before he could adjust or squirm away. At this point, another technician would attempt to quickly inject the sedative into the frightened and angry animal's leg, hopefully before they squirmed into a new position that made it awkward to make the injection. Most times we would have to reset the panel and try again with another attempt. Many times the needle painfully poked bone in the squirming monkey's leg. Occasionally, the whole syringe was grabbed out of our hands and thrown, or worse, chewed on while we reloaded. There was also a real danger that the leg was missed entirely and the injection could go into the chest cavity or abdomen—a potentially fatal mistake.

Once the injection was successfully given, a few minutes would have to elapse before it was safe to open the cage door. Frequently, a single injection wasn't enough to fully knock the animal down, but while they were still groggy and unable to move very well, we could open the door and safely give them a second dose. This was most often true with monkeys that had been around for a few years, as they had developed a tolerance for the drug. Like a heroin junkie, they required more and more of it each time in order for it to do the job. One monkey learned to fake his level of unconsciousness and as soon as the door opened, he would lunge out, very quickly, and very nearly sober. We learned to watch him carefully.

Once they were sufficiently sedated, there was a limited time with which we had to work with them before they revived. Again, the more experienced animals woke up much quicker than the others due to their tolerance of the drugs. Depending upon the procedure or study required, they would either be worked with right then and there (typically for vet exams or vaccinations), or they would be moved to another location. Most of the time we moved them to a new location. Regardless of how sedated they were, we held them from behind by both hands, each hand firmly gripping one of the monkey's upper arms and pulling them back behind his torso. In this way, even if he awoke a bit earlier than expected (and it happened a lot), he would be fairly well constrained and unable to easily escape or bite. I say "easily," because they did manage to escape from this grip on occasion, and in the case of one technician, bite. It was risky, but there were times where we had to move many monkeys in a short period of time (each with differing windows of wakeful versus unconscious states) and I had no choice but to hold one of these surprisingly strong monkeys in each hand. Walking briskly down the hall, I was always very thankful that they didn't wake up too soon. Most often the transport was between just two rooms—their regular colony housing and the metabolic room down the hall. It was the metabolic room where the research was most often performed.

We weren't the only group to use monkeys at the School of Pharmacy. Adjacent to our metabolic room were a couple of other rooms with monkeys. These rooms, like our metabolic room, had large windows in the doors, so it was easy to see the animals inside. It must have been a newer section of the facility as well, because the lighting and air handling was much better too. The monkeys in these rooms were beautiful light brown macaques. Much larger and quite a bit calmer than the typically hyper Cebus monkeys, they had an incredible look of wise sentience in their eyes, faces, and body language that could not be ignored. I felt fortunate that I didn't have to work with them. They were much too human-like.

I was familiar with metabolic cages for rodents, having used them before at Applied Lipids, but this setup was not at all what I expected. The well-lit room was about fifteen feet square and, compared to the regular colony housing, spotlessly clean. There was an uncluttered stainless steel bench top and chair near the door. A large squeegee on a wooden pole was propped in a corner near a neatly coiled hose on a hook. Another stout wooden pole was propped nearby. The large drain in the center of the floor was even shiny and clean. Like many of the other newer and cleaner animal rooms I worked in, the floor corners were all smoothly curved to prevent any debris from collecting. The whole place, while not exactly fresh, smelled much better than the monkey colony, despite being every bit as warm and humid.

What dominated the room, however, were the five large clear acrylic plastic boxes, facing each other on either side of the room. They were about three feet in all dimensions and a simple peg-and-hole style latch was all that seemed to secure their full-sized doors. The plastic used in these boxes was about an inch thick and numerous quarter-sized holes were drilled into all the sides and tops, while long vertical slits were cut into the doors. White nylon screws held the panels of each box together and other than the wheeled steel frame in which the base of each box rested, there was no other metal anywhere in or near any of them. They all sat low to the ground and I could see that each one had a plastic tray resting beneath thick round bars of clear acrylic that functioned as the floor. The trays were also made of this clear plastic, although it was only half as thick as the rest of the box's construction. Flimsy-looking, plastic framed mesh screens were neatly resting against one side of each box, with a couple of extra screens leaning in a corner. Upon closer inspection of the boxes, I saw a familiar setup—a false back wall. In this case, however, I couldn't see anything with which to pull it forward. Four two-inch diameter acrylic rods were in each corner, traversing from front to back, upon which the back panels seemed able to slide. The true rear panel of the box, behind the sliding panel, didn't have any holes, other than a single five-inch hole in the center.

These transparent metabolic chambers were custom made for this research group, and this was where our group earned its keep.

CHAPTER THIRTEEN

Metal Monkeys

The little monkey was never used for as many experiments as the other monkeys. The research technician in charge of keeping them healthy made a point of using him as little as possible, and she spent more time with this one in general. There was something about him that touched both of us in a way that none of the other monkeys ever did. Like most of the others, his eyes, facial expressions, and behaviors were fairly easy to read, so very much like that of humans. But unlike the behavior of the rest of the colony, which alternated between abject fear and violent hatred, his body language said submission. It was an unspoken but clear dialog of meek shyness, timidity, and possibly even affection. It was when he first held my finger that I discovered the closest thing I ever knew of another animal showing love in a truly human way. But while I may have only been imagining this love, his underlying expression of fear was also very real and never very far away.

Hereditary hemochromatosis (HHC) is a disease where the body accumulates too much iron due to accelerated iron absorption from the intestines. This causes severe damage to the liver and heart, and if left untreated, often causes cirrhosis and liver cancer. It predominately affects white males. Iron overloading is also possible in any person as a result of too much supplementation or a diet too high in the mineral, frequent transfusions or bleeding, or as part of another condition, such as liver disease. A traditional method of treatment was bloodletting, a procedure performed on the ill since antiquity. Despite bloodletting's poor results against most other diseases it was used against, in this case it was quite effective. In a modern setting, as much as half a liter once a week is drawn, which will bring a patient's iron levels down to normal. After this, monthly maintenance sessions are often required. For most people, however, a magic bullet in the form of a pill is preferred over repeated trips to a phlebotomist.

There are a few drugs available that do an adequate job of chelating (binding to) iron and allowing it to be flushed from the body. However, many of these are quite toxic in themselves. For example, when disodium EDTA was used instead of calcium EDTA, people died from an acute calcium deficiency. Even where toxicity isn't as large an issue, they usually require slow IV infusions over many hours on a frequent schedule in order to be effective.

A major benefactor to the university's medical school died relatively young as a result of hereditary hemochromatosis. Needless to say, both political backing and money for research was available to our group. The huge funding and support for research on chelating compounds was also the reason I was directed to do all the other intestinal studies, however ancillary it seemed. Both the disease and the chelator's mechanism of action involved how the mineral is absorbed through the intestinal wall. It was fairly clear to me now why my previous experience with rat and dog intestines was so interesting to them when my resume landed on their desks.

Most of the monkeys in the colony had been used on these studies for several years before I arrived, so I was just thrust into the ongoing experiments and shown what to do. For the most part, we were in the business of collecting monkey poop. That, and drawing blood, was the main focus of day-to-day operations with most of these monkey studies. It would be humorous in any other context: I was a member of a species with the most advanced mental abilities to have ever evolved on this planet—far surpassing those of any other species by nearly every cognitive measure—and my task was to scoop up the shit of my hairy cousins and place it into little cups. It's not that I felt some tasks were beneath me, but it reminded me of how I felt when scooping the cat boxes at home. When the cats watch me with a certain smugness in their eyes, I have to ask myself who the smarter species really is.

But context is everything and any amusement I got from the irony of the situation was soon forgotten, as I worked to get out of the steamy metabolism room each day as quickly as possible. These were not rescued cat companions who were dependent upon me for their survival. These were not wild and free animals whose feces

I was studying in the jungle in order to help monitor the quality of their natural habitat's nourishment. No, these were helpless prisoners who made it clear in every movement, grimace, and screech that they didn't want to be there and they wanted me to know it. They knew they didn't belong there. I could almost feel the heat of their hatred.

As with most animal studies where treating or curing a medical condition is the ultimate goal, the test subjects must either also have the condition or have something closely resembling it. In the case of our research in iron chelation, the monkeys needed to be overloaded with iron. Even though it was pretty straightforward, this was a lengthy process and had to be repeated to be effective.

The animals were anesthetized with an injection of ketamine and I started a slow IV infusion of saline. Over the course of forty-five to sixty minutes (often with additional injections of ketamine to keep the monkey sedated), I added iron dextran to the saline and it was slowly infused into their vein until about 750mg of iron had been injected. This process was repeated two or three more times, with each session separated by a couple of weeks so that their systems could stabilize to the additional iron. I drew blood during this downtime to calculate how much more iron could be safely added until they were fully loaded. Once loaded, the monkeys still wouldn't be used for at least two months until their final iron levels fully stabilized. They generally never needed to be reloaded again, once this whole process was complete.

A new iron study always began with my entering the colony and knocking out five monkeys, once the supplies and materials were assembled and readied for the task. An entire "monkey kit" was put together in a small plastic bin with a handle in the middle, the kind of tote that might be used for holding cleaning supplies. Syringes and needles were placed in a neat row, already loaded with the appropriate sedative, along with some extra syringes and sedatives. We always needed extras. Blood collection vials and their needles were in another section. A vial containing a drug to inhibit drooling, vomiting, and other side effects of the sedative was made ready for injection, in addition to paper towels, alcohol swabs, digital thermometer, and various other items that might be needed.

Each monkey had different durations for how long their sedative would effectively work. Some stayed unconscious for a long time, giving us plenty of time to complete our task, while others would only be under for a few minutes no matter how much sedative we gave, and even then, some wouldn't ever be under very deep. We tried to time it so that they were all down roughly at the same time, but it was never a smooth operation, especially with the more experienced animals. As soon as we had one sedated enough to handle and transport, he was immediately taken to the metabolic room. Walking down the hallway as quickly as possible, we frequently passed other researchers who would stop and stare at him as we passed. I remember feeling a sense of pride at those moments, thinking that I was important and lucky enough to work with monkeys instead of something as trivial, pedestrian, and boring as mice.

Holding the monkey out in front of my body, we quickly entered the metabolic room. Once inside, we weighed the monkey on a digital scale and a technician would then hold the monkey while I took their rectal temperature and drew blood. We used the same needles and vacuum tubes as phlebotomists use on humans. Rather than try to find a small vein in the arm or leg, however, I went right for the largest and most visible blood vessel available, the femoral artery. This large artery runs from the torso into the thigh and is the main source of blood to the leg. Conveniently, there is also very little fur in this location, so shaving was usually unnecessary. In a matter of seconds, a quick wipe with an alcohol swab was followed by a stick into the artery with the needle. The awkward insertion of the vacuum tubes onto the other end of the needle was something that took practice, but if all went well, in just a couple of minutes several tubes of blood were easily drawn for their various tests. A cotton ball was firmly pressed to the injection site, folding his little leg up to hold it, allowing a clot to form and preventing bleeding.

The technician would use this time to examine the monkey for any signs of injury or illness that needed attention. Often, there would be a little bleeding in their mouth as the cage-squeezing procedure would invoke them to bite the metal bars, especially the newer or younger subjects. The older animals learned that this cage biting was a futile response, but there was still a chance for injury. Once the animal was placed into his metabolic cage and the cage was locked, we headed back to the colony for the next monkey.

More often than we liked, a monkey wasn't down enough, or came up much too quickly. In many cases, they would simply be given more sedative, but usually we tried our best to instead rush through the procedures before they became too alert to handle. There were more close calls than there should have been. The main problem with giving them more and more sedative (aside from the monkey's safety and issues of increased drug tolerance) was that when they were loaded up with a large amount of these drugs, they would take forever to come back around. We had to babysit them until they did and that was an inconvenience. For this reason, we always had a magazine or a crossword puzzle in the kit.

With the flimsy screens slid into place beneath the floor bars of each metabolic cage and deionized ("DI") water provided from sipper bottles strapped to the outside, the monkeys actually woke up to something of a treat. Even though they were not going to have any appetite for a few hours, their normal (and certainly boring) diet of crunchy "monkey chow" biscuits was replaced with something that was presumably much more appetizing—or at least it smelled that way to me. Their food for the duration of the study was a thick fruity liquid, also dispensed from a large sipper bottle and tube. We called it a "monkey shake." The reason for this diet was because traditional monkey foods contained iron and since were we studying how much iron was excreted during the trial, we didn't want to introduce any new iron into their diet. This extra iron would have obscured the data and made it impossible to see how well the test chelator was working. The food was a liquid version of standard monkey diet, minus iron, and was prepared daily so that it remained fresh. Various oils, powders, and supplements were blended with DI water to yield a white liquid, not much different in thickness and consistency than a milkshake. Various fruit flavorings were added to increase palatability and each day they received a different flavor. The amount provided was based upon the animal's weight and the amount eaten was carefully monitored. Each day, the other technician would provide fresh food to the monkeys and the previous day's food bottles retrieved, while water bottles were topped off with fresh DI water. Our lab had its own water distillation and deionization system to ensure that no iron was introduced in that way either.

After a full week of the new iron-free diet in the metabolic cages, the actual study could begin. Now I knew what that large hole in the back of the plastic cage was for. I wheeled each cage away from the wall, allowing myself access to the rear, while the technician knelt in front of the cage's closed door. Instead of bars attached to the rear panel that I pulled from the front in order to squeeze the monkey, I used the wooden broom handle that was leaning innocuously in the corner to push the panel from behind. This was neither efficient nor easy to do. Not only was it difficult to slide the panel on its four corners, but the wooden handle would also often slide out of place and jam into the floor of the cage. The large wooden hole was too big to help keep the pole from shifting about. I was told that this system was not the original method intended with these cages, but it was the one we had and we just had to make it work.

The monkeys also learned to fight this plastic rear panel quite well and every attempt to squeeze them was always a case of the big ape trying to outsmart the little monkey. It was frustrating. They were so smart and so nimble, yet I couldn't simply use brute force. No amount of chest thumping on my part would make a difference. I just had to learn to be patient, quicker, and smarter.

Compared to their normal cages, the slots cut into the door on the front of these cages also made it much more difficult to inject the sedative. There was far less open space within those slots in which to line up a leg muscle for a clean shot. It also meant that if the monkey managed to get into the front corners, there was no accessibility at all and the squeeze had to be completely redone. Once the injection was completed, however, a few minutes would pass and the monkey could then be safely retrieved for his body weight, a blood sample, and drug dosing.

I loaded the test drug into a syringe, after having calculated the dose based upon the little guy's weight. Occasionally, it was given orally, but more often it was an intramuscular injection, ideally in the leg that wasn't just injected with the sedative. Unlike the rat's steel gavage needle, oral dosing for monkeys involved the insertion of a human baby's feeding tube. As with the rats, it was essential that the tube entered the stomach, not the lungs. Drawing back on an empty syringe once the feeding tube was inserted was a sure-fire way to be sure it was inserted properly. If liquid was drawn up, then we knew it was in the stomach. Given the high cost of monkeys, from both the perspective of time and money, it was crucial that a mistake was not made here. After dosing, we placed the monkey back into the cage and monitored him throughout his recovery from the sedative. It was important to note if the monkey vomited while waking up after receiving an oral dose. This was not just a concern during the recovery period, but also for several hours after dosing. It was not out of concern for the monkey's health, however. It was paramount that he received the full dose and any vomiting shortly after oral dosing would ruin the study and we would have to start over.

Assuming everything went as planned, the other technician (and myself on occasion) would then begin the glamorous routine of collecting the animal's waste. All of their feces and urine was collected every twenty-four hours for several days before dosing and every twenty-four hours for about a week after. This provided a before-and-after assessment of iron clearance.

Upon sliding the screen out from beneath the floor bars, a plastic spatula that looked very much like a large, rounded dinner knife was used to scoop and scrape the monkey feces into a plastic specimen cup. The feces' consistency was always some combination of soft, runny, and hard, depending upon the individual monkey and his stress. Whatever the shape of the poop, it was always a disgusting and disagreeable task to collect it, and every morsel of dung had to be collected. As the monkeys peed, their urine passed through the screen into the tray beneath. The tray sat at a slight incline with the low spot at the right front corner, into which was affixed a small tube. Each day, the one-liter sample jars with varying amounts of urine were removed and capped, and new empty jars were placed over the end of the tube. All the sample containers were labeled, weighed, and recorded. Once back up in the lab, the technician sterilized the urine and feces in an autoclave to kill microbes. The collected feces was mixed with deionized water into a homogeneous soup, freeze-dried, then a measured amount of the poop-powder was reconstituted and any undigested particles removed. Finally, a chemist would analyze it and the urine to determine the relative amount of iron contained in each. Any iron discovered in a sample was the result of the chelating drug's effect. One of the five monkeys was an untreated control and therefore no iron would be detected in his waste.

Often, I also drew blood during the study, sometimes as frequently as once or twice a day.

At the end of the study, usually after a week, the monkeys would be knocked down one last time for their blood and weight and then returned to their normal cages with the rest of the colony.

In the three years that I worked for the School of Pharmacy, there were very few weeks that we didn't have a monkey metabolic study running. Because we didn't allow the normal caretakers to have access to this room, we were responsible for its cleanliness. This meant that it was always much cleaner than it would have been otherwise. During studies, the trays and filter screens all had to be cleaned immediately following the daily sample collection. This generally involved spraying them down with DI water, ensuring that no feces remained stuck to the screens. Invariably, urine also spilled onto the floor because of the awkward and somewhat haphazard way that the collection bottles were attached, so the floors also had to be hosed down. After a study was completed and before the next one started, the cages were given a much more thorough cleaning by the other technician, using high-pressure water from the hose. Once everything was spotless, she gave the cages a final complete rinse with DI water to ensure there would be no residual iron remaining from the tap water. Finally, the large squeegee was used to push everything down to the drain in the center of the room. This cleaning task was a very unpleasant, steamy one, as the room's normal ambient temperature and humidity matched that of the colony housing. During cleaning, however, the relative humidity was probably well over 80%.

While the metabolic studies were a primary task performed on a regular basis to determine relative effectiveness of a test compound, frequent pharmacokinetic studies were also performed for these compounds as well. What these studies did was show us what happens to the drug as it makes its way through the body over time. Once again, monkeys were sedated in the colony (after having been fasted for about sixteen hours prior) and brought into another room for the procedure. This time, however, we brought them into a different torture chamber.

The animal facility had a large surgical suite that remained dark and unused for the most part. Our group probably used it more than any of the other groups while I was there, but even so, it seemed that it was only ever used once a month. There were seven operating rooms total, two of which were being used for equipment storage. Of the other five, three were on one side of a dimly lit central hallway and two were on the other, those two being separated from each other by a sterilization and supply room. Multiple hand washing stations and supply carts lined the hallway, as well as cabinets containing surgical gowns, gloves, masks, and beard/hair bonnets. All the rooms had doors closing them off from the hallway, but the remaining three rooms were conjoined. They were only divided from each other as required, by drawing closed large and dingy folding panels mounted into tracks on the ceiling. One of these three were the rooms we always used.

The operating room was very much like what you would expect for humans, but without the sterility. An adjustable table was in the center, a table clearly made for humans. Above it was a large movable parabolic lamp and to the side, a couple of stainless steel rolling trays for instruments. At the head of the table was the anesthesia machine, with its associated dials, gauges, tubes, gas tanks, and waste-capture canisters. It looked to me like it was surplus equipment from a hospital rummage sale, as the dials were old (the numbers partially worn off) and a couple of the glass gauge covers were cracked. A few mismatched rolling chairs were nearby, one of which was broken. The institutional-looking clock on the wall was always off by several hours. Many of the tiles on the walls were cracked and a few were even missing. At least the large crack that traversed the concrete floor had been sealed at some point in the past. I wondered whether or not I was really in one of the top twenty research universities in the US.

Since our normal procedures were non-invasive, and unless there was another group performing surgery nearby, we never closed the doors to the operating room. We didn't even scrub our hands at a sink first. The primary reason for our use of this room, rather than any other normal procedure room, was for the inhalation anesthesia that was available. These monkeys were going to be down for a long time, much longer than what was safe or effective with injections of narcotics. Often, we did this study on a couple of animals at once, so we also left the room partitions open and used both tables at the same time.

Occasionally, however, another group would perform procedures in other surgical suites. Sometimes it was sheep, and other times goats. Rarely, I would even hear the squeal of a pig. One time, while bored during a monkey study, I poked my head into the door of another room where a sheep was propped up on her back, as if in a reclined sitting position. Her skull had been cut wide open and sections of her brain had been removed, while multiple electrodes and computer leads were dangling out of her head. The researchers were measuring data that somebody clearly felt was important. She was unconscious, fortunately, and the tubes in her throat and legs were keeping her alive for the duration of whatever horrid things the humans were doing to her. While I was relieved to learn that this was a terminal study and she would never wake up, my thoughts at the time focused more on the fact that, compared to monkeys and rodents, it must be difficult to dispose of such a large body as hers.

Once our room was set up with all of our equipment and supplies and the gas was hooked up and ready to go, we retrieved a monkey. Using as little injectable narcotic as possible in order to not complicate or compound the effects of the anesthesia gas, we brought the monkey into the room. Still half alert and only groggy, the immediate task was to intubate him with a breathing tube. Normally used for infant humans, this somewhat flexible plastic tube had a small, deflated balloon at one end and at the other was a standard breathing hose connector, along with a second, much smaller tube that attached to a syringe. Inside the primary tube was a stiff plastic-coated wire that was used to help keep the whole thing rigid during insertion. Holding the tube against the chest of the monkey, I used a Sharpie marker to indicate to what depth the tube would be inserted, roughly judging where the trachea split into the main bronchial tubes. The infant breathing tube must be inserted into the trachea without going too deep. I made the mark on the tube at the point where the monkey's lips would be.

I used an illuminating tongue depressor to help with the insertion process, but it was never easy. After applying a glob of K-Y Jelly to the rounded tip, I inserted the breathing tube into the mouth and, with some difficulty, negotiated past the epiglottis to finally enter the trachea. This was much harder than inserting a feeding tube into the esophagus, and the scraping of the breathing tube's tip against the tracheal cartilage was not a pleasant feeling. I had to work fairly quickly as well, because with the stiffening wire still inside the tube, there was little room for air to flow through. I couldn't begin to imagine how unpleasant it all was for the semi-conscious monkey. Once in place, however, I depressed the attached syringe, inflating the little balloon that both sealed any gap in the trachea and also helped hold the tube firmly in position. Upon quickly withdrawing the stiff wire, I then attached the hoses from the anesthesia machine. The hoses had a valve attached that allowed a gas and air mixture into the lungs, while the monkey's exhalations left through a separate tube into a waste-scrubbing canister that captured the gas. This way, the room didn't fill up with noxious gases and cause us all to fall asleep (or worse). Nonetheless, the leaks from these old machines were unmistakable to my nose, and posed an occupational hazard that we willingly chose to ignore. The hum and hiss of the anesthesia machine was always present in my ears and we almost always worked in silence.

Then we laid the monkey on his back on the surgical table. We had previously placed some surgical towels over a heating pad filled with recirculating warm water in order to help maintain his body temperature; we were going to be here a long time. I smeared K-Y Jelly on his eyeballs and eyelids to keep them from drying out, and likewise for his lips and tongue, which would frequently be sticking out around the tube. To further ensure that the tube remained in place, I gently tied strips of gauze around the breathing tube and then around monkey's head and neck. While I did this, the other technician shaved the back of his calves to allow easier access to the veins there. The obligatory jokes about his shaved legs were made. After lubricating a urinary catheter, I inserted it into his penis, again using one intended for infant humans. Sometimes, especially on smaller monkeys, getting it to pass beyond the prostate posed a challenge, but eventually, with some degree of frustration and coaxing, it went in. I then collected the pre-dose urine by attaching an empty syringe to the catheter and gently pulling the plunger. Disconnecting the syringe from the catheter for a moment, I transferred the urine to one of the dozens of labeled vials, repeating the draws and transfers until the bladder was empty. Then I flushed the bladder with saline and drained it a final time. Leaving the catheter in place with the empty syringe attached, I repositioned the monkey to lie on his side, making sure that his breathing apparatus wasn't kinked or pulled too taut.

Finally, I inserted a butterfly needle into the small saphenous vein on the back of his calf and taped it into place with bandage tape. This IV was from where I would draw regular blood samples, the first sample being taken before dosing. On a regular basis, one of us would insert a digital thermometer rectally to ensure that the monkey didn't become too warm or too cold during the long procedure. We usually covered him up with a small hospital baby blanket.

Sometimes, the saphenous vein on his leg was insufficiently healthy or large enough for drawing blood and I would have to find a new vein. If the monkey had been used for similar studies before, there was often scarring on the vein, which made it difficult to insert the needle properly. Likewise, there was occasionally extreme difficulty inserting the catheter through the penis due to scarring or other issues causing a narrowing of the urethra. The best I could do in those circumstances was to hold the penis firmly (not easy with K-Y Jelly on my fingers) and literally force the catheter tip all the way in, cringing the whole time. Apparently, I was able to feel a morsel of empathy when it came to tormenting their genitals. The catheter didn't have far to go to reach the bladder (only a few inches), but I always inserted it several more inches into the bladder to ensure that it didn't slip back out over the course of the day. Not only was the catheter left in place for convenience, but it also effectively blocked the urethra, preventing a steady leakage of urine from escaping the monkey throughout the procedure. That urine, along with his blood, was what we were there to collect.

Sometimes, I dosed the unconscious monkey with a single quick intramuscular or intravenous injection of the test drug.

Oral administration was also not uncommon. Often, however, I performed a slow intravenous infusion. In the case of the slow infusion, a mechanical syringe pump was used, allowing the drug to be injected at an extremely minute and steady rate over the period of a full hour. This was done because of particular clearance and metabolism aspects of the drug, but occasionally it was done because of the acute toxicity that would have been observed in a sudden full dose. IV drug administration was always done in the other leg than the one used for blood sampling.

These were all-day studies. Somebody had to continually stay with the animal in case there was an emergency, with myself or another technician popping in and out between our other tasks to relieve each other. There were rarely any complications, and for the most part, the time between the many blood and urine draws was usually spent with the assistance of paperback books and crossword puzzles, occasionally getting up to check their temperature and anesthesia levels. For most studies, I collected blood and urine at thirty minutes post-dose and then every hour after that for the following eight hours. Each time, the urine was fully drained and the bladder was flushed with saline. I placed the blood in various types of vials for later analysis and I immediately spun some of it in a small centrifuge we set up in the operating room, separating the serum from the rest of the blood for yet other tests. In addition to testing for the drug's metabolites, other standard blood tests that were performed included complete cell counts and full chemistry profiles that allowed us to monitor the health of the both monkey before and after the dosing, in case there were any changes caused by the drug.

Once the study was over, we turned off the anesthesia gas and removed the breathing tube, while the animals were allowed to recover. This was done with a lot of patience and close monitoring because different monkeys wake up differently. Some recovered slowly and calmly, while others panicked and even after lying there quietly, would suddenly jump up in a drunken, agitated state. I could see in their rolling eyes, various degrees of wakefulness, and as they were able to focus, they became more and more physically active, trying to sit up or roll over. Once they started writhing a bit more noticeably, it was a mad dash to carry them to their home cage before they became too physical and hurt themselves or one of us.

In one case, a monkey did come around much more quickly and suddenly than anticipated and he threw himself off the table, falling three feet before crashing onto the hard tile floor. Before we could catch him, however, he was off and running, drunkenly climbing onto whatever fixture was available in the space, slipping and falling, knocking equipment down, screeching the whole time, and scaring us quite a bit in the process. I knew he was scared too, but this was an embarrassing loss of control on our part and that took over as my main concern at the time. After ensuring that the doors were secured and while I stood guard to hopefully keep him away from more danger or destruction, a net was finally retrieved by the other technician. After a great deal of chasing him around the room, we eventually caught him and returned him to his cage. Fortunately, he didn't injure himself or us, but it was certainly a lesson for us to watch them even more closely as they regained consciousness. Most importantly to me at the time, nobody else witnessed this near disaster.

Sometimes, the monkeys never woke up. On purpose.

When a drug was found to show a great deal of promise, its relative toxicity to organs had to be established. The only way to effectively do this was to take the organs out and examine them. Usually, these toxicity studies involved my injecting the monkey with many doses of the drug over a period of days or weeks, always collecting blood and urine in the process. On the final day of the study, I gave the animal a fatal IV dose of pentobarbital. This was usually done in the necropsy room.

The necropsy room was adjacent to the incinerator and its sole purpose was to be the location to cut large animals into small bits. The gore involved was probably why the window in the door was always covered with a taped-up piece of paper towel. The room itself was not large, perhaps fifteen by twenty feet. Tall cabinets lined one wall, stuffed with preserved tissue samples from other research groups, stored for reasons unknown, perhaps forgotten. The back wall had a stainless steel counter, a large double-basin sink, wall-mounted pump bottles of soup and disinfectants, and a paper towel dispenser. The other wall had more cabinets and a doorway leading through a small alcove that passed into the incinerator room. Dominating the room and secured to the center of the floor, was the dissection table. Stainless steel from top to bottom, this structure was about two and a half feet wide and four feet long. It was illuminated by a large, adjustable surgical lamp suspended from the ceiling and had a sink built into the far end with a flexible spray hose. The working surface consisted of eight perforated stainless steel panels that covered a shallow basin beneath, which sloped to a central drain. With the panels in place, blood and other fluids could drain into the basin, keeping the animal relatively clean. A faucet handle on the side controlled how much water could continually wash over the full surface of the basin, keeping it relatively clean and easy to wash when the necropsy was complete. This table was a simple setup, however. The more elaborate tables have electric waste disposals in the drains (identical to what is in most kitchens) and drafting fans to suck away all noxious odors. With our table, we had to manually dig out the small bits of flesh that got caught in the drain trap and the smell was sometimes overwhelming once the intestines were cut.

As with toxicity studies in other species, most of the organs were harvested. However, since new monkeys were incredibly expensive, especially to use in a terminal study such as this, not a single organ was ignored. Once I began the tissue harvesting, the list always seemed longer than I remembered, no matter how often it was followed. Typically, it included liver, spleen, lung, pancreas, bile, kidney, adrenal and salivary glands, vein, heart, cartilage (from trachea), bone marrow (from femur), bone (rib), thymus, diaphragm, bladder, testes, prostate, skin, tongue, lymph node, muscle (leg), esophagus, stomach, three parts of the small intestine (duodenum, jejunum, ileum), large intestine, and colon. Another technician would label sample vials and check off each organ on the list, as I used a pair of scissors to cut a sample piece from each organ and placed it within its own vial. Cutting up the testes was unpleasant, as was using a pair of diagonal cutters to crunch open the femur to extract marrow, but few things disturbed me about this process as much as cutting off a piece of the monkey's tongue.

When we were done, we cleaned and sanitized the back counter and sink and removed the disposable covers on the lamp handles. We scrubbed the dissecting table, panels, sink, and basin with disinfecting soap, cleaned and dried our instruments, and finally sprayed everything down with ethanol. The remaining unwanted pieces of organs and the rest of the carcass was double-bagged and then casually thrown into the chest freezer in the incinerator room. That young little monkey was now trash.

Rarely did we perform these terminal studies on any of the older monkeys in our colony that we had been using for our other long-term experiments. New animals were purchased instead for these toxicity and other short-term experiments. Because it was difficult at times to procure these monkeys, whether wild-caught or captive-bred, we found that, occasionally, they were too young to use right away; we had to house them for a little while until they matured. Since our regular colony was full, we used another smaller room with portable cages. Arboreal monkeys never like to be housed low to the ground; they only feel secure when they are in the trees, looking down. However, since these portable cages were considered "temporary," the animal's long-term mental well-being wasn't a major consideration. These monkeys were never going to live very long, unlike the insane and older boys in the regular colony.

I did not like going into that secondary colony room if I didn't have to. Despite everything I did to monkeys for a living, it still made me sad to see youngsters come into this environment. They were all so very young and they were all so very scared. I think it was easier for me to work with the older and seemingly angrier monkeys. I knew that they hated me. On the other hand, these little guys just seemed scared to death—all the time. I must have had a conscience after all.

CHAPTER FOURTEEN

Metal Dogs

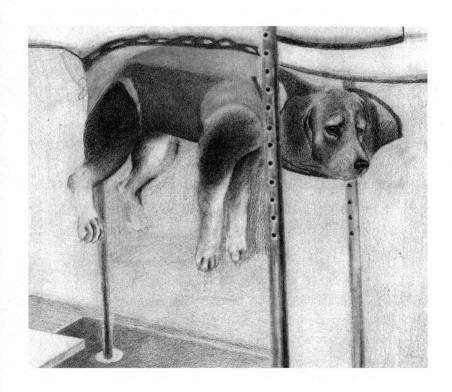

Just barely enough pentobarbital was loaded in the syringe. Because I had only enough for one injection, and my supervisor, who held the key to the lockbox where the barbiturates were stored, had gone on vacation (and it was the weekend as well), it had to be done right the first time. The beagle was originally given a test compound that we had given up on, so he was to be destroyed since he was unusable for any other research. Unfortunately, because he was squirming so much and I was in a hurry, I missed his vein. The barbiturate went under the skin, enough to make him groggy, but it was far from a lethal injection. In fact, it turned out to be just enough to make him mostly unconscious. In a moment of utter stupidity, I decided that using dry ice held near his mouth would be the next best thing to use to finish him off, since I was in the privacy of the kennel anyway and had some handy. After many minutes of this, however, he still did not die. Finally, I took him to the CO_2 box in the incinerator room, laid him inside, and turned the gas on. After thirty minutes, this finally did the trick. Gassing dogs and cats with carbon dioxide at shelters was legal in many states, but it was against the policy of the School of Pharmacy. I never told anyone about the situation with this dog, as it would have been embarrassing. I wasn't usually so sloppy with those kinds of procedures and I felt horrible about this botched kill. It would have made me look incompetent, which was clearly the most important issue to me at the time, but I did feel a little bit bad about the whole thing.

Before a new drug can be tested in humans, the Food and Drug Administration require that toxicity first be established using two different mammal species. One must be a rodent (most often rats or mice) and the other species most commonly used is the dog. The reason dogs are used more frequently than other species, such as monkeys, is price, availability, size, and temperament. Monkeys are very expensive to acquire and house, they aren't always available when you want them, and they are not very friendly to work with. Dogs on the other hand are relatively cheap, live in a standard kennel, are easily handled, and are happy to see you, even if you are coming to inflict suffering and death. Beagles are particularly amenable to being victims.

There was a lot of prior research showing the efficiency of chelators in the rat, and the research group I was in had already established the data for the use of monkeys. However, it was also clear that monkeys and rats couldn't be compared very well for the purposes of toxicity. There were just far too many differences. In the case of the iron chelators, however, the use of the dog turned out to be problematic also. Some compounds that were well tolerated in rats and monkeys were highly toxic in dogs. Because the primary investigator didn't want potentially effective and human-safe compounds to be rejected outright simply because dogs were not tolerating them well, he decided that dogs would also be iron-loaded and tested for iron clearance as well. Thus, we began working with beagles.

While monkeys were somewhat alien, rather exotic, and certainly dangerous (not to mention more than a little scary, at least to me), dogs were familiar, happy, easy to handle, and normally thought of as our friends. I really didn't look forward to the dog studies because of my previous work with them and because it was going to be more difficult to look them in the eyes. Even though monkeys are vastly more intelligent than dogs, many years of my familiarity with dogs as pets formed a bond between us that I would never experience with the monkeys.

It's possible that the scary, dangerous, and insane nature of the monkeys made it even easier for me to perform studies on them. It was almost as if by my knowing that, given half a chance, they would rip my face off, it made it somehow easier to inflict this sanctioned suffering upon them. With one exception, they weren't my friends and only wanted to harm me. This didn't make me more aggressive in dealing with them, but it probably ensured that I felt little remorse at the time.

That was not the case with the dogs.

There were many events during my time as a vivisectionist that may have planted the seeds to my becoming compassionate. It simply took too long for them all to be connected. I admired monkeys for their high intelligence and advanced social organization, and thought it was absolutely fascinating that humans evolved from a related ancestor. I knew rats and mice were smart too. As a kid, I marveled at TV shows and documentaries about rats. I loved them as pets long before I went to work in the field. I honestly do not know why there was such a disconnect between my seeing them as beloved pets and my turning them into suffering victims. Likewise, for dogs. I always had one or more pet dogs in my home, for as long as I can remember. But I never made the connection between the dogs I worked on in the lab and those I knew and loved at home. Perhaps since the beagle was a breed that I was mostly unfamiliar with it helped me keep an emotional distance. If I had to work on a breed (or mutt) identical to the friend that I had at home, I don't know that I would have been able to remain so distant. It was clear to me that I must not grow attached to any of them, however. I simply could not engage that part of my brain and heart and still function in this job, so I left that part of my humanity at home.

The process for iron-loading dogs was very similar to that of monkeys, in that the iron had to be infused slowly over the course of a few hours and repeated several times. Rather than anesthetize the dogs, however, they were docile enough to work with while awake. A sling made specifically for dogs was used. This was comprised of a strong nylon mesh fabric, suspended between four sturdy upright posts mounted on a platform. The mesh had holes cut for the legs to be inserted, as well as a cutout section allowing access to their penis. Their torsos were thus supported fully and they hung suspended in the sling, with their legs dangling in the air. Another section of mesh fabric was also fitted across the top of their torso and affixed with Velcro. This top section was pulled snug and prevented them from being able to squirm their way out of the sling. For the most part they rarely struggled, but because the procedure took so long, they would become bored and eventually want to be let out. For this reason, they were usually given generic Benadryl to pacify them.

After shaving their forelegs, I inserted and taped down a butterfly needle and started a saline IV drip. I also inserted a urinary catheter to periodically withdraw urine; otherwise, the large volume of fluids being infused would have quickly made their bladders very uncomfortable. Once the infusion was going for a little while and with the antihistamine in their system, they usually nodded off and slept through the entire process. It was very hard for me to stay awake as well. Good thing I had my crossword puzzles and a paperback.

Dosing was also easier with dogs, as they didn't need to be sedated or restrained. They readily swallowed capsules, tolerated injections, and if it weren't for the occasional slow-infusion pump studies, the slings would not have been used for dosing at all. When it came to collecting blood and urine as part of multiple pharmacokinetic time points on the other hand, slings were again indispensable for restraining the bored and often stubborn beagles. They quickly became used to the slings and any contact with humans was still preferable to sitting alone in their kennel, even if it was in the form of unwanted restraint. Otherwise, most blood and urine samples were easily collected with the assistance of a technician holding and distracting the dogs, while I inserted needles and catheters.

The dogs were supposed to be played with and given exercise on a regular, daily basis, but I never really witnessed it happening, since there was no yard or other outside space for them to go to. I suspect it consisted entirely of them being let out one at a time into the little kennel space in front of their runs, while a caretaker hosed down their kennel, only to be returned again shortly before the next dog run was cleaned. This was only done once a day. However, on some studies, they got to take something of a little field trip.

Cardiac toxicity is a real concern for many drugs, and the iron chelators we tested were no different. On a human, it's possible to easily attach a portable ECG heart monitor and read the results from it. On dogs and monkeys, it's another story entirely.

They did not like to have anything attached to them for very long and our monitors required at least eight hours at a time to get the full results. While there were Kevlar jackets that could supposedly be fitted to monkeys that would allow a heart monitor to be attached, it was problematic at best. Either the little Houdinis were able to take it off or they were able to extract the electronic monitor or its leads from within. In either case, they simply destroyed the equipment, potentially hurting themselves in the process. We did have one monkey who was willing to wear a jacket with the ECG monitor (he's pictured on the cover of this book), but he would have been the only one. All the others that we attempted to fit it on were brutally opposed to it and literally fought tooth and nail to remove it. With only one usable monkey and no desire to try it on any of the others, we had nothing else to compare the data to, so the attempts at using monkeys were aborted. Dogs were going to be our only hope for this source of data.

Any time animals larger than rodents had to be transported to or from the animal facility, it had to be done in portable steel cages. The cage units had to be sturdy and rugged enough for the large macaques that were used by other groups, but they also functioned to move dogs and smaller monkeys as well. The robust nature of these heavy three foot by three foot wheeled boxes were far in excess of what was required for the dogs, but they served their purpose. They were solid, cold gray steel on all sides with only a few inches of barred opening around the top of the walls. The lock on the door was hefty. When the macaques were being transported into the facility, I could see their fingers holding the bars, while they gazed out at me with an unmistakable expression of fear in their eyes. That was all I could see of them. Little fingers and nervous eyes, as they were trundled out of the truck and down the halls to where they would be housed until the day they died.

A heart study consisted of five dogs, each animal with their own leash and a clipboard holding their paperwork. The beagles were not entirely happy to be put in these boxes either, but with a little coaxing (that is to say, a certain amount of lifting, pushing, and shoving) they eventually obliged, proving the inherent stubbornness of this particular breed. It felt rather silly to use these hefty rolling cages to transport a half-dozen dogs, as the thick-gauged ruggedness was certainly overkill for this species. One by one, I pushed their dull steel boxes down the halls to the loading dock, where they were lined up in the hot Florida sun.

The loading dock should have been called the "smoking dock," because it seemed that there were always more animal caretakers taking breaks out there than there were inside cleaning cages and feeding animals. Nevertheless, the plain white, unmarked cargo truck was there awaiting our load, idling with its own noxious smoke filling the air. I don't think that truck was ever adequately maintained.

The driver was a cheerful and hyperactive, chain-smoking "good ol' boy," who loved nothing more than to talk about his adventures on the local racetracks, where he dreamed of one day racing for NASCAR. I learned more about car racing from him than I ever wanted to and it made sense that he was hired as a truck driver for the college. With his help, the cages were loaded and I climbed up into the tobacco-stained passenger seat for the short drive to the veterinary college. He remarked that he preferred these trips with the dogs. He felt the sheep and goats were OK too, but the pigs smelled too much and always required that he hose out the truck afterward. It turned out that the university did a lot of research on farm animals too, even though I never saw much of it. In hindsight, I'm glad I didn't.

A short trip a few blocks away from our dirty loading dock found us in front of the vet school, with its nicely manicured lawn and attractive landscaping. Rumbling up to the curb, I was acutely aware that the image of these ugly and heavy cages with mysterious and unknown occupants, being pushed by someone in a dirty white lab coat, must have looked fairly out of place. Especially when compared to the pampered house cats and toy poodles that are usually carried down that sidewalk.

Unloading the heavy cages two at a time on the truck's hydraulic lift gate was an adventure. There was barely enough room for both boxes and me, and my attempt to hold them and prevent them from falling three feet to the pavement was precarious at best. To make matters worse, the half-broken lift was never really level, so I was fighting hard against gravity each time. Wheeling them into the vet school was almost surreal. After being in the enclosed, windowless space of the subterranean animal facility, it was jarring to suddenly be working in clean, brightly lit, windowed veterinary space. Young vet students in their scrubs and exuding optimistic love for kittens and puppies bustled about, casting curious glances at me in my grungy white lab coat standing next to the dungeon-like cages now lining the hall outside a procedure room. I felt self-conscious and had to take a quick glance to see if I had any old blood stains on me, as I didn't always wear the newest lab coat when working with the often-messy dogs. Perhaps they wouldn't notice the dark red stains.

A veterinary technician helped pick the first dog up and put him on the table. The dogs would always tremble. Not only was the excitement (fear?) of the journey stressful, but as they have never really been off the ground before, the height of the exam table was also quite troubling to them and their nervous behavior was obvious. The heart monitor was about the size of a paperback book and had half a dozen electrical leads attached to it. The vet attached those leads to the beagle's chest in prescribed locations, while I helped hold the dogs still. A new nine-volt battery was then inserted into the device and turned on. Inside was a standard cassette tape that captured the digital data. When the monitoring was to be finished at the end of the study, this tape would be removed and returned to the veterinarian for analysis. The entire ECG monitor and all the wires were bundled onto the dogs' backs under the colorful and slightly sticky gauze tape known as "vet-wrap." Almost their entire torso was wrapped in these brightly colored bandages and the vet and techs always commented about how "festive" the dogs looked. They looked more annoyed than anything, in my opinion.

I always felt guilty with my research animals at the vet school. I was sure that most of the students were judging me for doing research on what the more curious of them called "poor puppies," as they peeked in and petted them. I felt the research was important at the time and whether I imagined it or not, I didn't like to be judged in such a negative light. I do admit that I was jealous of the students, though. I had at one time entertained the thought of becoming a veterinarian.

Ironically (or perhaps not so ironically, in hindsight), my supervisor kept a dozen dogs in her small condo, which she regularly trotted out at dog shows in the hope of winning ribbons or trophies. I learned that she kept them in small crates all day, only letting them out, just a couple at a time, to play once each day. Her place was small and therefore she kept the dog crates stacked like large bricks. I remember thinking that this was no way to keep dogs, and I told her so, not recognizing the hypocrisy of my feelings when compared against what I was doing with dogs for a living. She would laugh it off and then complain about how they were "all pains in the ass" anyway, as if they deserved being housed that way. I never visited her home, and I'm glad. I always pictured it being every bit as messy as her office-lab.

Finally, the research dogs were returned to each of their rolling metal cells for the truck ride back to the lab. At least it was something new and different for them. The incidental "enrichment" of riding in the back of a dark truck was better than nothing and it never occurred to me that they might also enjoy some walking and playing on the grass alongside the vet school parking lot. I doubt that the dogs had ever felt grass under their feet, but that wasn't something I thought about at the time. I had a job to do and the driver was sitting in the idling truck, chain-smoking cigarettes and awaiting my return. Enrichment wasn't part of my job, in any event. It was something other people were responsible for providing. Enrichment was something that all non-rodent lab animals were required to receive, but it wasn't required from me. Besides, I had been continually warned against making friends with these animals, a warning I readily heeded. I was going to be killing each of them, after all.

Sitting in the kennels again, I devoured more paperbacks while I listened and watched to make sure none of the dogs were tearing at their wrappings. Other than the untreated control, I had already delivered one or more doses of the test compound and any heart anomalies would show up on the ECG's cassette. I was to keep them calm and sedate for the duration. More often than not, I had to enter a dog run to re-wrap a dog who managed to quietly extricate himself from the bindings. They did not care for this bulky and strange attachment and there was always one who was a pain in the neck about it. Nevertheless, they were happy to have me in the kennel with them and they merely wanted to play while I was trying to reattach their device. I never played with them because it was far too easy to get attached.

Despite my job and despite my ability to turn off the switch of empathy that allowed me to do my job, I really wanted to help some of these dogs. I knew that they were needed for our research, but so many of them were needlessly killed at the end of a study, when they could have lived out their lives in a happy home instead. Adopting them out should be easy, unlike the insane, exotic, and dangerous monkeys. Unfortunately, I found out that it was not as easy as I had assumed. When I inquired about it, my supervisor told me that it wasn't possible. When I asked why, I was told that there were few people who wanted them and that there would be too many questions regarding their source. The Powers That Be at the university research facility did not want it to be known to the public that dogs were used in research. Therefore, the public would not be able to adopt the dogs. I finally was able to get one adopted, but only because he went to the home of another employee of the animal facility. I didn't even find out who that was. I was told that it was futile to attempt any more adoptions and I finally gave up trying.

All of the dogs who went to the vet were monitored for heart irregularities, but the toxicology research wasn't complete without tissue samples. With the exception of the one who was adopted out, nearly all of these dogs were killed and had their organs harvested, exactly as described for the monkeys. Because irritation at the injection site was an issue for many of the drugs injected, the skin tissue from that location was an additional sample taken. Again, it was the tongue that made me squirm the most during necropsy. I do remember once cutting out the os penis (the penis bone) so I could see what it looked like and add it to my collection of skulls and bones. My curiosity and academic interest in mammalian osteology wasn't deterred by the morbidity of that moment.

We would often have music playing during the necropsy. One time, I thought it would be funny to play a song by Ogden Edsl, called "Dead Puppies." It was a song that was considered darkly humorous and it was highly requested on *The Doctor Demento Show*. I don't know why I thought it would be funny to play during a dog necropsy. I guess I was being "edgy" and irreverent—perhaps in an attempt to laugh away the horror of what I was doing. Nevertheless, it wasn't long into the song before I realized that I had made a horrible mistake playing it. My coworkers were not amused and I turned it off, feeling quite ashamed of myself. It was not one of my proudest moments.

Dead puppies aren't much fun
They don't come when you call
They don't chase squirrels at all
Dead puppies aren't much fun

My puppy died late last fall
He's still rotting in the hall
Dead puppies aren't much fun, no no no
Mom says puppy's days are through
She's going to throw him in the stew
Dead puppies aren't much fun

CHAPTER FIFTEEN

Dirt Monkeys

I peeked into the colony to see why it was taking so long for my co-worker to return. She was violently hollering at the monkeys at the top of her lungs, shrieking at them to "shut the fuck up!" I don't know why she had a meltdown with them, but it was almost as if something had snapped in her. When she saw me enter, she stopped yelling, grabbed her equipment, and hurried from the room. I asked her about it later and all she would say is that they were getting on her nerves.

As I look back upon my history in this field, I am appalled by how little negative emotion I felt at the time about the work that I did. Certainly, there were moments of dismay when I was performing mass killings. I never did like that at all, especially if the animals were never used. I was still under the impression that animal research was a valid and important aspect of good bio-medical science. If I used an animal in an experiment, it was a regrettable, but necessary death. However, if the animal was never used and then killed, it was a much more unfortunate waste of life. It's ironic to think that I considered torturing an animal first to be the preferable action!

Another aspect of this job was the expectation that I would not allow emotions to cloud my work. In fact, the requirement that researchers should never be biased by emotion permeates all fields of science, and in most contexts, this is appropriate. Whether through ridicule by my peers, or simply as a logical-sounding admonition by a supervisor, I was to remain impartial and unattached to the animals that I was working on. This pressure to produce a dissociative worker is also seen in both medicine and military, as a technique to distance the person performing the act from the act itself. Furthermore, by focusing on the larger and loftier goal (in my case, a cure or treatment for disease), I was also able to indulge in a certain degree of moral absolution, a feeling that I am not morally corrupt for performing these acts.

Not all of our group's research at the School of Pharmacy was derived from existing internal projects. A neighboring state had contracted with us to do some research into their dirt—the dirt in a children's playground to be specific. It seems that there was some concern about the amount of arsenic discovered in the soil of a playground that was built atop the site of an old lumber mill. For many years, wood was pressure-treated there, making it poisonous to termites and other wood-destroying insects. While they no longer commonly use arsenic in this process, there was concern that the soil had remained hazardous to little Johnny when he slid into home plate during a Little League game. Our youngest monkeys were thought to be the perfect animals upon which to test the bio-availability of the arsenic in this dirt.

A lot of time and effort (as well as expense) were put into iron-loading our colony of monkeys. Since we were able to procure new monkeys for other short-term and terminal toxicology studies, it was not very disruptive to use those same young new arrivals for the arsenic studies. We also already had the metabolic cages that would be required. What we didn't have was experience with the type of dosing that would be done.

The procedures were very much the same as with the iron chelators. Five monkeys were fasted and placed into the metabolic cages. They were dosed with arsenic, while blood and urine samples were taken at specific time points, including a series of hourly time points while under anesthesia in the surgical ward. Following this, they were kept in the metabolic cages for four additional days, where their urine and feces were collected and analyzed. Fortunately, none of the monkeys were killed for these studies.

What was traumatic, however, was the dosing. While one of the monkeys (the control) received a simple oral dose of arsenic in water, the others would receive a thick slurry of actual mud. This mud was a mixture of water and the soil samples that were provided to us from various contaminated sites. Even at the time, I couldn't believe I was actually doing this. I was force-feeding dirt into monkeys.

This never worked very well. First of all, we learned quickly that they would have to be given an anti-emetic injection to keep them from immediately vomiting the dirt upon awakening. The goal was obviously to have them pass the dirt through their systems in order to determine if any of the dirt-bound arsenic was absorbed through the gut. Early into these trials, however, we discovered that nearly every monkey who was force-fed the dirt would vomit upon awakening. This was not really surprising, since the sedative itself was nausea inducing, but it was even more of an issue with the dirt as compared with the usual drugs that we gave them in other studies. Nevertheless, even the process of dosing itself was highly problematic.

The soil samples were initially screened and filtered by a chemist to ensure that the particle size was quite small, less than 250um. This fine dirt, when mixed with water, would still separate quickly, with the soil rapidly precipitating and settling into a dark layer on the bottom of the vial. I therefore had to continually shake the vial while loading a syringe in order to draw up a consistent dose. Even then, I had to continually turn and shake the syringe in an attempt to keep the soil suspended. Once it settled, it created a solid plug in the narrow neck of the syringe and there was no way to force it out.

As with all oral dosing, I inserted a feeding tube into the mostly unconscious monkey. I then quickly attached the syringe, always turning and shaking it, and tried to depress the plunger. Once I succeeded in getting all the dirt into his belly (always after several messy and unsuccessful attempts), I injected some water to flush out the feeding tube and syringe. I then moved on to the next victim, until all the test animals received their doses. The total amount of dirt in each dose was about one teaspoon, but the actual amount was calculated beforehand to provide one milligram of arsenic per kilogram of body weight.

Fortunately, the amount of arsenic ingested was never enough to become toxic, because adequate clearance time was given between any duplicate tests that were performed in the same monkey. Furthermore, through these studies, it was confirmed that arsenic bound up in dirt is far less bio-available than free arsenic in water, so neither they nor little Johnny were ever in any danger of being poisoned by the dirt. While the dirt-fed monkeys certainly suffered torment in these trials, at least they were not killed as a result. Instead, they were later used for other studies where they were tormented and killed as required.

My laboratory animal skills were used for many other studies, even when I was not directly involved in the research—for example, a particular neurological study that required monkey brains. After doing the dosing and euthanasia (and any other task required for these studies), I removed the monkey's head. Because skin would impede the task, I also skinned the heads, pulling their scalp over the skull from behind, after making an incision. The face was attached very firmly at each of the orifices, so I had to cut it away from the eyes, nose, lips, and ears. I was keenly aware that this was identical to how a hunted animal is skinned for taxidermy too, but I wasn't interested in cleanly removing the skin, as it would soon be disposed of. Finally, I took a rotary skull blade and cut the cranium open to extract the soft gray tissue within.

The brains needed to be kept as intact as possible, so pliers were almost always required to break away parts of the lower skull, with bits of bone and blood occasionally flying off and sticking to my lab coat. The extraction of the fragile brain tissue was fairly difficult, especially as the brain stem is so deep within the skull, but finally I retrieved the brain and gave it to the researcher who wanted to do the analysis. Occasionally, they would want the eyeballs too, so I had to remove those from the sockets. Eyes are actually held in place by some of the body's strongest muscles, and their removal is a lot harder than it would seem. In addition, removing eyeballs is not for the squeamish. In the end, I was left with an unwanted body, an empty shell of a head, and a bloody mess to clean up. The whole task was not really too different from the rat brain extraction I performed in my dad's basement for my girlfriend's school project, exactly twenty years earlier.

CHAPTER SIXTEEN

Reformation

I loosely followed a vaguely Buddhist path before I became vegan, but both philosophies blossomed in me almost simultaneously, as I saw that the logic in one closely paralleled the logic in the other. The Five Precepts are primary suggestions for all Buddhists to follow and are a main tenet in every single school of Buddhist teaching, from Zen, to Tibetan, to Theravada. They are not commandments or laws, but rather commitments to abstain from harming living beings, stealing, sexual misconduct, lying, and intoxication. The first tenet is clear and unambiguous: we should not harm other living creatures. This originated from a concept that is central to Buddhism, Hinduism, and Jainism: the concept of ahimsa, *which means literally, "to do no harm."*

If one word sums up my moral baseline, it is ahimsa.

All beings fear danger,
life is dear to all
When a person considers this,
he does not kill or cause to kill.
—*The Buddha, the* Dhammapada

All in a day's work.

It seems weird to look at it that way now, but that's really how it was. Why would I even question it? Using animals as a tool to develop treatments and cures for human disease was an unfortunate, but essential, part of business. And I was part of that business eight hours a day, five days a week, fifty-two weeks a year. It paid my rent and satisfied my desire to work in science. I was a skilled specialist in a high-tech field. It was simply how things are done and I was proud of my abilities to do my job well.

I have since learned that lab animals make horrible proxies for humans in biomedical research. None of the studies where I spent so much time and money destroying animal lives had ever resulted in any cures or treatments for disease or other afflictions. Those lives all went to waste. I'm really not sure how I could have been so blind for so long, though. In looking back at my childhood, it's rather easy to see why I looked at most animals as somewhat less worthy of compassion than humans. Certainly, being raised in a home where mice and rats were regularly raised and killed to feed snakes was no small part of that mindset.

Just like the person who eats animal flesh without a single thought of where it comes from, or ignores that an individual creature with feelings and a lifetime of suffering was the source of his meal, I was also not thinking too much about the lab animals as individuals. There were just so many thousands of identical rats and mice, with seemingly no other purpose but to be used as cogs in the glorious human machine. After all, they were bred specifically for this purpose and they knew nothing of any life in the wild. How could they possibly miss it? Instead of individuals with thoughts and feelings, they were more like little mindless cloned machines that I needed to poke, prod, slice, and manipulate. Of course, I was aware of their desire to avoid pain and like most all of the other researchers I met, I truly tried to minimize their suffering, but the real problem was that they were all just a means to an end. Whether that end was a full cure for disease or just symptom relief, or whether it simply part of my day's work attempting to earn a paycheck, when compared to my goals, the importance of their lives was entirely and completely insignificant.

It was always about me.

I think the ego is really where the crux of the issue lies. Everything was always about me. My paycheck, my job, my experiment, my research results, etc. This is really no different than the mindset of a meat-eater—their hunger, their plate, their taste buds, their convenience. In fact, it defines most typical people in American society: their horseback ride, their bacon and eggs, their leather boots, their circus lions, their purebred show dog, their insect-free yard. I really don't think that it's a case of not caring at all about animals.

Instead, I think it's a case of caring so much about one's own self that everything else becomes immaterial. Their ego's importance and well-being may stretch so far as to include compassion for their loved ones (and pets), their community, or even their country, but anything non-human that is either in the way or can be used as a tool to reach their goal, is considered disposable and worthless once that utility has been used up. It doesn't matter whether it's animal, vegetable, or mineral—the sense of entitlement to consume them without restriction almost defines the modern human.

As a secular Buddhist (a Buddhist who doesn't accept the supernatural claims of religious Buddhism), I learned that one of the most fundamental things causing our own suffering is our strong attachment to the concept of "self." According to Buddhism, since nothing at all is ever permanent and everything continually changes, there also cannot be a permanent self or ego. While the philosophy behind that teaching warrants entire books of its own, the basic warning against a preoccupation with one's self is still valid and relevant in modern, non-Buddhist society as well. The terms "self-centered," "self-absorbed," "egotistical," and "conceited" are all commonly used to negatively describe a person who is primarily concerned with themself. Society has warned against this behavior since prehistoric times. In Greek mythology, Narcissus was a beautiful youth who fell in love with his own reflection, leading to disastrous results. The evil queen in the Snow White fairy tale was also obsessed with her beauty, as she frequently summoned the mirror to reassure her. In this tale, it did not end well for her either. Vanity and pride is even described as the primary reason why Satan fell from Heaven.

Empathy is one result of looking beyond one's self and one's own desires. When we stop focusing on ourselves, we have time and energy to look at others and consider their needs. Empathy for other humans is relatively easy, since we can readily identify with them. Empathy for the animals we bring into our homes is also easy, since they have become extensions of our families, even being called by many (myself included) as their "furry children." So why does empathy end when we think about the laboratory (or the slaughterhouse)? I believe there are two reasons for this. Individuality and invisibility.

When we look at a single animal, whether an ant on the walk or a beloved house cat on our lap, we tend to ascribe human characteristics to it. This anthropomorphism is a primary reason why we feel empathy for individual animals. We like to think, for example, that our lap cat loves us and showers affection upon us and we take joy in giving affection back in return. My sister, an avid horse-rider, was quite adamant in her insistence that her horse loved to be ridden and showed his appreciation and love in countless ways. We like to imagine the ant as industrious and single-minded, devoted and purpose-driven. We avoid stepping on her, because we tend to see her as a tiny individual with her own thoughts and a goal in life. On the other hand, when a giant ant colony has invaded their manicured yard, most people don't think of the thousands of individuals in the same empathic, humanized way. They see them as a group. Even the most callous person may consider the act of a child burning an ant with a magnifying glass to be repugnant, yet they will paradoxically be quick to pour poison on that very individual's anthill which contains "pests" that must be destroyed. Similarly, a kitten filled with playful joyous exuberance is a delight to both adults and children alike. We take great pleasure in watching it grow and we share in a life of companionship and affection. How do we respond to a group of feral cats roaming around our neighborhood at night? Do we see them as the playful kittens they once were? Do we see each of them as individuals who might have shared our home and our lives, given different circumstances? It's more likely that we see them as a nuisance and immediately call for animal control to come pick them up. We conveniently ignore the fact that once this is done, they will often be destroyed—behind closed doors.

It's our quickness to decide that violence is the best way to deal with groups of animals that reveals our callous disregard. Anybody who has spent any time with a single cow, chicken, or pig (at least those that haven't been mistreated) will know how very smart and affectionate they are. Even fish will display personalities and a range of behaviors that we would describe as somewhat intelligent and self-directed, once we observe and interact with them as individuals and not as a mindless collective.

Before becoming vegan, I had chickens who I kept around the yard for their eggs. I had raised these girls from chicks and they were so tame, they would fly up to roost on my shoulder. They came running to me anytime I came outside, even when they had plenty of food and I brought no treats. They would let me pick them up and hold them. They would settle on my lap and doze off. For all intents and purposes, these were pets. Every bit as loving, affectionate, playful, and smart as any dog or cat I ever had.

Our neighbor at that time had a lonely young steer that they were raising for slaughter. Every day, I would go out to the fence between our yards, and he would run up full gallop and suddenly stop on a dime, right before me, and give me a snort. He loved to have his head and face scratched and he seemed to value the time I spent with him. As I walked away, he would moo loudly and follow me along the fence, hoping I would come back. The family that was raising him cautioned their children to not become fond of him and to not spend any time with him. They knew that if they did become friends with the steer, they would become attached to an individual and would be crushed (as I was) when he was slaughtered. I really enjoyed spending time with that cow and those chickens, and I would never even think of causing any harm to any of them, yet at that time, I still readily ate meat from the grocery store.

Which brings me to the second reason why we are so readily able to ignore the horrible plights of many animals: invisibility. We may or may not know if the shelter is a no-kill, but we will tell ourselves nonetheless that the cats rounded up by animal control will find new happy homes. We may love the chickens in our yard, or the big friendly cow next door, but the plastic-wrapped chunks of meat at the grocery store aren't those animals. In fact, they aren't animals at all anymore. They are now called by names that disguise what they really are. They are now "veal," "roast," or "sirloin." They are "pork," "ham," "bacon." They are merely chunks of "meat," not even referred to by a description as identifiable as "muscle" or "flesh." They were certainly not "that cute cow that lived next door" or "that playful chicken who followed me around the yard."

Former Beatle, Paul McCartney famously said, "If slaughterhouses had glass walls, everyone would be a vegetarian." That lies at the heart of why we are able to turn off our empathy. When we can't see the victims at all, not only do they stop being individuals, but they even stop being animals altogether. They become "things." This is exactly why there are so many new "Ag-gag" laws on the books, suppressing the rights of people to film and expose the cruelty found in factory meat operations. This is why universities and research company labs are so very secretive and have high levels of security around their facilities. Out of sight, out of mind. These industries rely on that invisibility being maintained and they spend millions of dollars each year to keep the curtains closed. This is why you don't see many books such as this one. This is exactly why it's so important to open those drapes, to shed light on the machine behind the curtain. It's vital to expose the Great Wizard of Science for what it really is.

* * *

Paradigm Shift: *A fundamental change in approach or underlying assumptions.*

One would think that after so many years of my torturing and killing animals, the light bulb of compassion would have blinked on much sooner. The clues were all there, but I was still under the illusion that animals were nothing more than unfortunate, but essential commodities. However much I thought I loved animals, at least as wildlife and as pets, it's clear now that I was just like every other typical person when it came to exploiting them for utilitarian purposes or for my own pleasure. It wasn't until I discovered veganism that I saw how using animals and animal products permeates nearly every single aspect of our modern lives. I was shocked.

I knew about vegetarianism, but I always considered that simply a dietary choice, not an animal rights decision. People became vegetarians for their health and for no other reason, as far as I knew. It never appealed to me because I liked the taste of meat and that was that. We evolved to eat meat, after all, right?

I was also opposed to cosmetics testing since the early 1980s when I first learned of it, but I really only thought about it as a part of makeup manufacturing, and as a male, it seemed to have little to do with me. I naively ignored the fact that I used soaps, shampoos, deodorants, and other animal-tested products purchased from these same companies. I also knew that I didn't like the idea of hunting or fishing, but I really didn't think about it too much either. Those were activities that others engaged in and they didn't have much impact on my life. It never occurred to me to look at it from the animal's perspective, and I believed the population control lies that were regularly put forth.

I realize now that the industrial uses of animals are kept very well hidden from the general public. Because we are not raised to question too deeply how and why our modern conveniences and foods are created, I feel my ignorance of those practices was somewhat excusable—especially in a pre-internet society. But now that I *do* know, there is no turning back. How can anyone with any amount of compassion who learns about the horrors simply shrug and turn away from it? How can they keep using these products and perpetuating the brutality now that they know?

Empathy. The same emotion that originally turned me away from eating veal and to support whales was the key. It took me a while to wake up and kindle a sense of empathy, but once I started down that path, the transition was surprisingly rapid.

Strangely, I went straight from an all-meat Atkins diet to become an ovo-lacto vegetarian almost overnight. After leaving the School of Pharmacy and moving to New Mexico to follow my wife's new career in engineering, we found a whole new group of friends. We had them over to our house regularly, and like most Americans, the barbecue was a typical way of entertaining guests. One of our friends was a vegetarian and while grilling her veggie burger (she had to ask me not to grill it under dripping meat, which didn't even occur to me), I asked her why she was vegetarian. She just looked at me with an exaggerated sad face and said she just felt bad for the animals. I didn't pursue it further and she didn't press the issue, but that moment stuck with me and I pondered it later. Why didn't *I* feel bad for the animals too?

Since moving from Florida, I was no longer working in the field of pharmaceutical research. This was because there were no jobs, not because I wasn't interested in doing it. However, that lack of job opportunities forced me to readjust my career path. I worked for a while doing really fun and interesting ecological research for the biology department at the University of New Mexico. When that grant dried up, I worked as a quality compliance auditor for a pharmaceutical pill and vial filling company. I probably would have continued along those lines if a home business selling public domain movies on the Internet hadn't taken over the next ten years of my life.

I used Atkins to lose a lot of weight during this time. About thirty pounds quickly melted away from my body over the course of a few months and I was maintaining a weight that I liked. I ate nothing but meat and an occasional vegetable, but since the Atkins book said this was perfectly healthy and I felt ok at the time, I never questioned it. Even after I quit the rigid prescription of this diet, I still stayed very meat-centric. A typical meal, even after I stopped Atkins, was to plop an entire pound (or more) of ground beef on my George Foreman grill and when cooked, slather a half-inch of mayonnaise across the entire top of that blackened slab of flesh. A few ribbons of mustard with some salt and pepper and it was done. Yes, it is disgusting for me to describe that now, but it's a big part of how I ate for several years. All my other meals during this time were at least 75% meat. It was not unusual for me to fry an entire pound of bacon and eat it in one sitting. I bought into the Atkins myth that meat was my friend and ate fast food several times a week, often skipping the bread and fries. I was a carnivore extraordinaire long before the term "carnist" became known.

But then something switched in my head. I don't know exactly what it was that triggered the change, but I think the fact that I was now raising alpacas, sheep, and chickens had a lot to do with it. We got the alpacas and sheep for their fiber (my wife spun, dyed, and wove yarn) and the chickens for eggs and scorpion control. I became pretty close friends with the incredibly personable and smart chickens and somewhat friendly with the sheep (as much as they would let me). The alpacas were also mostly friendly and I started breeding the one fertile female we had.

It was at about the same time we had our first baby alpaca that I began thinking a lot more about what I was eating and I was starting to feel guilty about it. I remember reading in one of my "How to Raise Alpacas" books that I shouldn't eat meat before interacting with them, because they would smell it on my breath and therefore think of me as a predator. This would presumably make them harder for me to handle and control. That really made me stop and think. The sheep and the alpacas were such gentle creatures, true herbivores, and here I was, a big ugly carnivore, breathing death into their nostrils each time I interacted with them.

I do have an occasionally impulsive nature. One day, while looking into the large and wary eyes of my pet livestock ("pasture ornaments," my friends called them), I decided then and there that I was going to be a vegetarian. My decision was rather sudden, even surprising myself, and when I told my friends, their response was laughing sarcasm, "Yeah, right." It might have been their reactions or it might have been something else, but my mind was now firmly made up and I realized that my resolve was actually strengthened by their gentle mocking.

I still didn't really make the connection between my former work as a vivisectionist and this newfound empathy for animals. I was still under the impression that animal research was a necessary evil, and while I would certainly no longer engage in it, I was glad that others still did. How else would we get more medical advancements?

To be honest, I wasn't really sure if I would be able to become a vegetarian, so I started off slowly. I decided that I would give up all pig products first, since they are incredibly smart. It's been said that they are the smartest non-primate land animal—as smart as a four year-old human. How could we kill and eat something that was nearly as smart as some of my friends, I joked? After a week or two of not eating pork (and not really missing it), I decided to include cows as an animal I would also no longer eat. That too went very well. Very soon thereafter, when I began to struggle with the decision about what animal should be given up next, I suddenly realized that it's not intelligence that I should be focused on, but rather whether or not they suffer. I figured why not just go all-out and drop all birds and sea animals from the menu as well. I was now a full-fledged vegetarian!

That lasted all of two weeks.

But it wasn't the lure of meat that I left vegetarianism for— quite the opposite, actually. I had decided that as a vegetarian, I would need to make sure that I got all the nutrients my body required. I was still eating eggs and cheese, so I felt confident that I was getting enough protein, but just in case, I had better look it up online. Well, it wasn't long before I also took a look at what the "radical" concept of veganism was about. I was shocked at how extreme it seemed to me at the time. No milk? No cheese? No eggs? No gelatin or honey? No white sugar?! How could I possibly eat anything at all?

Most importantly, however, I learned that veganism wasn't even about food! It was about true compassion for all animals. At that point, I realized that by focusing on my dietary needs and desires, I was actually missing the big picture. I was again thinking about my desires, my self, my ego. Veganism was entirely about respecting animals. Period.

After a couple of hours of research online, I finally reassured myself that a vegan diet was not only able to meet my nutritional requirements, but was actually the healthiest diet that I could have. The hell with vegetarianism; I was going to go vegan! If my friends were surprised before, they would be shocked now. I didn't care. This was important; this was real. This was a game changer for me. I immediately stopped eating my chickens' eggs and swore off cheese and the rest of my dairy addictions. It took me a lot of research and a lot of swearing at how much animal product was in nearly every package of processed food. I quickly learned that if I was going to be a healthy vegan, I had to start preparing my foods from the whole raw ingredients found in the produce aisle, not in the boxes of toxic waste found in the rest of the store. I was going to get healthy whether I wanted to or not.

Food I could figure out easily enough. The rest of the vegan equation was going to be tougher, though. I had a lot of leather (I rode a Harley-Davidson, after all). My shoes, belts, and jackets were leather, but the thought of climbing into the skin of another being was repulsive to me now. My sweaters were wool. I had a couple of silk shirts. All of this had to go, sooner or later. I ended up selling some of it, giving some of it away, and donating the rest to thrift stores. My closets went through a purge. But the animals roaming my three-acre backyard were another story. How could I be a vegan and "own" livestock? What do I do with all of the chickens' eggs? These questions were not as easy for me to answer. Especially since I was now on Facebook and had made a lot of new vegan friends there. How could I explain it to them?

When I quit smoking cigarettes at the School of Pharmacy over fifteen years ago, it was one of the most difficult undertakings I could imagine. I had tried many times before to quit, without success. I tried slowly weaning myself off of them but my lack of willpower doomed that method. I also tried quitting cold-turkey many other times, but as soon as life became too stressful, I quickly relapsed. Finally, with the assistance of the relatively new (and expensive) nicotine patch, I gave it another go. Despite all the warnings to the contrary, I still went to my old smoking haunts and hung out with my smoking co-workers and friends every hour as I used to do. The difference was that I was now wearing a patch and eating sunflower seeds.

The seeds were helpful in that they provided plentiful hand-to-mouth behavior, just like smoking. They gave me oral stimulation, just like smoking. Most importantly, though, by going out and having a regular "seed break," I was still benefiting from the social interaction and getting out of the lab for a mental and emotional break, just like smoking. I had to give up cigarettes, but I didn't have to give up everything else about the habit that I also liked. I'm not sure whether I consciously meant to do it or not, but I also became incredibly obnoxious to my friends and coworkers about how bad their smoking was and how wonderful I was for being a non-smoker. In order to avoid the personal humiliation of failure, my ego guaranteed that I would succeed. And I did.

Similarly, ten years later, both on Facebook and with my local friends, I made a big deal about how I was vegan. I collected many vegan friends and joined dozens of vegan groups. I "liked" countless vegan pages and gave myself a vegan nickname. Again, whether I meant to do it or not, by being so public I helped ensured that I wouldn't backslide. I even had the word "vegan" tattooed on my wrist—a very public and permanent announcement of my commitment. I learned a lot about veganism in a very short amount of time and wondered why I hadn't done it sooner. Why do people find it so hard to do? I wasn't really worried about whether or not I would stay vegan, as going back to the way I was before wasn't even on my radar, but I was worried about how to avoid being hypocritical about the animals in my care. How do I explain them?

It turned out that I needn't have worried. Most of the vegans I met online also had to struggle with issues and items from their past. Some of them even had chickens. I was apologetic about the animals, and didn't mention them too much. It was one thing to care for rescues that needed a home (such as all the cats and dogs in our house), but the livestock were animals that I purchased specifically to exploit. Definitely not a vegan thing to do and I was not happy about it. The problem ended up resolving itself eventually. After a couple of tough years where my wife was laid off and my business profits dried up, I knew that I couldn't afford keep them any longer. The alpacas and sheep were sold and the chickens were given to a good home. It's not something that I'm happy about to this day, but I really had no other choice at that time. Our house had entered into foreclosure proceedings.

Since then, my veganism is as strong as ever, although I do eat too much vegan junk food. I find myself doing once-strange things, such as rescuing bugs in my house instead of killing them and mourning the death of a bug when it hits my windshield. I created and administrate the largest vegan group on Facebook (*Vegan Humor*, with over nearly ninety thousand members at the moment and growing fast), as well as several other popular vegan-oriented groups and pages. While I'm not the most vocal or prolific in my vegan outreach, and I have a tendency to be rather inflammatory against those who continue to exploit animals, I decided to write this book as the best way in which I can positively affect animal rights progress in society.

When I announced the book on Facebook, I was basically "coming out of the closet" as a former vivisectionist. This horrified me because I had thought long and hard about whether I would write under a pseudonym or use my real name. I still don't know if I made the right decision. After all, who would want to have something like this permanently attached to their name as a top result of a Google search? I wasn't worried about burning any bridges professionally, because I have no interest in ever working in that industry again (although, I would still like to find work in ecological or environmental research someday). However, the problems of writing under a nom de plume are many, so in the final analysis, I felt it was best to simply use my real name. Time will tell how wise that was.

I knew that some friends would be horrified to find out about my laboratory past and I expected to receive some negativity. However, the vitriol wasn't from any of my friends, online or otherwise. Instead, I received the angry responses from strangers who not only considered me to be the lowest form of scum to ever have walked the face of the Earth, but who also wanted to see great misfortune fall upon me as well. Their anger was palpable and just barely stopped short of death threats. I was a little shocked at first, since these were people who were so vocal about showing compassion to other animals, yet could very quickly show so much violence towards another human—one who openly admitted his mistake. I realized quickly, however, that in the face of the horrid realities of what these industries and I had performed on innocent animals, people needed to lash out. They simply needed a focus for their quite justifiable anger and I had presented them with a convenient face and name. This is especially true when the enormous pharmaceutical industry is already monolithic in its faceless and impenetrable refusal to budge on the issue, despite public outcry against it and the solid scientific refutation of these practices.

In the heat of their anger, the term "scapegoat" comes to mind and I might complain about that, except for the fact that I am indeed guilty of their accusations and a part of me feels strongly that I deserve such animosity. As I mentioned before, I'm not seeking everyone's forgiveness, but I do ask that they consider their own pasts. I ask them to consider the fact that they used to eat meat, eggs, and dairy, all the while blindly (or apathetically) supporting the cruel and inhumane atrocities regularly committed upon pigs, cows, chickens, turkeys, sheep, and fish. I ask them to consider all the makeup and toiletries they once purchased that paid for people to torture countless rabbits, dogs, and other sentient beings. I ask them to consider all the leather or fur they wore, contributing to a market that is not just a side-product of meat, but is actually an industry that frequently tortures and kills animals for just that one product. If those angry people can come to forgive themselves of directly contributing to those horrors once they discovered a more compassionate lifestyle, perhaps I can also be allowed to wake up to my own new life of compassion, and perhaps be forgiven.

I never made a lot of money as a vivisectionist. I earned, at my peak in 2000, a little over thirty thousand dollars per year. At fifteen dollars per hour, I only earned what many people are now saying should be the current minimum wage. I owned fifteen-year-old cars that were always breaking down and lived in small two-bedroom apartments, eating ramen noodles, Hamburger Helper, and cheap fast food like most of the low wage earners of our society. Just like in the majority of other industries, upper management in pharmaceutical research earns the bulk of the payroll and I was certainly nowhere near their level of income. If any of the ire against me is for supposedly profiteering, that ire is focused so far down that particular ladder as to be laughable. I was merely surviving. The way I earned money to pay my bills was not admirable at all, but it was not lucrative either. As it is, I still live in a small two-bedroom basement apartment, earning minimum wage from the part-time jobs I'm able to find. However, if I do ever earn any money in the future, I would like to open an animal sanctuary focusing on those species who are typically used in research and cosmetics testing. It's the very least I can do.

Interestingly, when the topic of animal testing is brought up, a lot of people express the wish that prisoners—in particular, pedophiles, rapists, and murderers—should be the subjects of pharmaceutical testing, instead of animals. I can fully understand the emotional innate desire we have to exact a violent revenge upon the most violent and despicable members of our society. We all have some part of us, large or small, that believes an "eye for an eye and a tooth for a tooth" is fully justified. However, we need to step back and realize that creating *fewer* victims, not more, should be our goal. The industry is certainly despicable and corrupt in the way it exploits our small furry cousins, but that does not in any way mean that it should be allowed to be despicable and corrupt against somebody different instead. Rather, violent and depraved criminals, while still kept apart from society, should be considered mentally ill and effective treatments for them should be sought, even if it often seems futile. It's inconceivable that in the twenty-first century, we would simply warehouse them behind bars, or worse, perform torture upon their bodies or minds. The goal for all of us should be to reduce suffering for all beings in this world. This simply cannot be done by acts of vengeance.

It wasn't until many years after working as a vivisectionist that I learned that the whole industry of animal research is built upon a foundation of willful ignorance, barbaric insistence on antiquated assumptions, and a perpetual need to maintain the status quo, "because that's how it's always been done." This illusion of necessity is funded quite well, of course, by the corporations and institutions interested in maintaining the profit stream earned at the expense of millions of lives. Exorbitant prices are charged for the few drugs that *do* work, in order to fund the research that only yields an 8% success rate. Naturally, they also seem to focus primarily on treatments for symptoms, never a cure, as this perpetuates their profit stream.

Ironically, one of the minimum-wage jobs that I have been forced to take, since my career in research was derailed, was a pharmacy technician position at a retail giant. I witnessed firsthand how so many people are taking dangerous drugs (sometimes the very ones I had worked with in the lab) without any knowledge of what they do, how they interact with all the other drugs they are taking, or how many animal lives were destroyed in their research and development. Sadly, most doctors are ignorant of many of those details as well, often simply prescribing whatever some pharmaceutical representative urged them to prescribe. Frequently, these patients I met (including a very famous former NFL football player) had to turn away medications because of their high cost, even with the help of their meager insurance coverage. The industry claims that the high cost of medicines is warranted because they need to recoup research costs, conveniently ignoring that their investment costs would plummet if they hadn't wasted huge sums on pointless animal studies. Most ironic, however, was that the majority of the illnesses and conditions for which I dispensed medications were due to poor diets heavy in animal products. We therefore torture and kill millions of other animals in the attempt to find treatments for diseases that are caused by eating animals in the first place. It's a vicious cycle.

The traditional way to fight this system of torture is to expose it, to make it widely known to the average person, and to force elected officials to recognize that our votes and our campaign dollars will not flow their way until it is stopped. Even that is not enough, however, considering the fact that most politicians are firmly in the pockets of these same giant corporations. Our political pressure should certainly still be applied, but until we put enough financial pressure on the institutions that profit from the abuse, little will change in Washington. We must make it clear that we also will not buy the products that are the result of animal testing. Corporations care only about money, so that is the language that must be spoken, loudly, clearly, and with enough numbers to be felt in their wallets. Veganism is part of that boycott, by definition, but even most vegans are unaware of the massive scale to which animal testing has grown. That needs to change, urgently.

There are many animal rights groups that focus on animal testing, exposing the horrors and abuses as they are discovered. One of the more successful groups is Stop Animal Exploitation NOW! (SAEN). Using legal action with (and sometimes against) the United States Department of Agriculture (USDA) and the National Institutes of Health (NIH), SAEN has successfully exposed and ended cruel university programs from coast to coast.

Another example of a group that has made a tangible difference is the Beagle Freedom Project (BFP). This nonprofit group, formed as a service of Animal Rescue, Media, and Education (ARME), focuses their mission on rescuing, rehabilitating, and finding homes for beagles (and other species) that have been officially released from research and testing labs after years of torment and isolation. Their rescues have taken place all over the world, including Korea, Spain, Hungary, and the UK, as well as the US. However, not content to simply be an adoption group, their founder and animal rights attorney, Shannon Keith, has also spearheaded legislative action to require that labs release dogs and cats to adoption who would otherwise be destroyed. So far, California, Nevada, Minnesota, and Connecticut have all signed bills that require this action. Not satisfied with only state-level enforcement, BFP is now taking this to the national level, hoping to present a similar bill to Congress soon.

There are also many other smaller groups equally committed to exposing and ending such abusive research, each one of which fights a tough legal and financial battle against extraordinarily powerful interests. Even so, our voices will not be heard or taken seriously unless we also present a rational and clear path to a solution. Organizations such as the Physicians Committee for Responsible Medicine (PCRM) have done an amazing job of using verifiable facts and solid research to highlight the scientific and medical fallacies surrounding animal testing. They have been instrumental in getting the use of animals reduced or eliminated in many institutions, including medical schools.

Other groups have also been looking at unique ways to get the message heard and to help end the suffering. The White Coat Waste Project focuses entirely on the use of taxpayer money, drawing upon bipartisan collaboration to attack animal testing from a purely financial perspective. According to their website, the US government alone wastes over twelve billion in tax dollars every year to pay for wasteful, painful, and ineffective animal experiments.

They urge people on both sides of the political aisle to expose and eliminate the waste by holding the animal abusers accountable.

By supporting organizations such as these, either through donations or volunteer efforts, our voices will be heard that much louder and change will occur that much quicker. Leafleting, protesting, and engaging local politicians and policy makers are always helpful and will add tremendously to the base of active support in your community. Government and industry want to shut our voices down, but as long as it's still legal to speak up, we must continue to do so and never stop until the last cage is empty.

Yes, I *was* a monster. I am far from perfect, as there is no way to completely avoid making choices that may harm other beings, but I try my best. I know, however, that I will never again work in or directly support an industry that exploits animals. Even though I am very ashamed of my history and what I did to so many animals, I do sincerely hope that this meager effort at writing my horrible story will make a small difference in the lives of a few animals not yet born. In the lives of those beings who will only know life in a laboratory cage, tormented by countless chemicals and horrid diseases. Animals who are forced to submit to the infliction of pain unheard of in even the most brutal and long history of human tortures. Animals who deserve to be free of misery. Animals who deserve to be fought for. Animals who deserve a voice. Animals who deserve better.

RESOURCES

General Information

1000+ Doctors Against Vivisection by Hans Ruesch, 1989 (free eBook)
www.malzoism.org/downloads

Doctors and Lawyers for Responsible Medicine
www.dlrm.org/about.htm

Maximum Tolerated Dose (Film)
www.maximumtolerateddose.org

Medical Research Modernization Committee
www.mrmcmed.org/Critcv.html
www.mrmcmed.org/Critical_Look.pdf (eBook)

Physicians Committee for Responsible Medicine (PCRM)
www.pcrm.org

Industry

American Association for Laboratory Animal Science
www.aalas.org

Animal Welfare Act
www.aphis.usda.gov/animal_welfare/downloads/awa/awa.pdf

"Guide to the Care and Use of Laboratory Animals" (1996, National Academy of Sciences)
www.nap.edu/openbook.php?isbn=0309053773

Legal

Animal Legal Defense Fund
www.aldf.org

Lewis and Clark Law School, Center of Animal Law Studies
http://law.lclark.edu/centers/animal_law_studies

Activism

American Anti-Vivisection Society (since 1883)
www.aavs.org

Beagle Freedom Project
www.beaglefreedomproject.org

Coalition for Consumer Information on Cosmetics (CCIC)
www.leapingbunny.org

Cruelty Free International (formerly "British Union for the Abolition of Vivisection" / BUAV)
www.crueltyfreeinternational.org

Eurogroup for Animals
www.eurogroupforanimals.org/what-we-do/category/animal-testing

Humane Society International
www.hsi.org/issues/biomedical_research

New England Anti-Vivisection Society (NEAVS)
www.neavs.org

People for the Ethical Treatment of Animals (PETA)
www.peta.org/issues/animals-used-for-experimentation

Physicians Committee for Responsible Medicine (PCRM) Action Alerts
www.pcrm.org/raa

SAEN - Stop Animal Exploitation NOW!
www.SAENonline.org

Safer Medicines
www.safermedicines.org

Sanctuary (Film)
www.thisissanctuary.com

Stop Vivisection: a European Citizens' Initiative (ECI)
www.stopvivisection.eu

Alternatives to Animal Testing

Alternatives to Laboratory Animals (ATLA)
www.atla.org.uk

AltTox.org
www.alttox.org

American Fund for Alternatives to Animal Research
www.alternativestoanimalresearch.org

European Centre for the Validation of Alternative Methods (ECVAM)
http://ihcp.jrc.ec.europa.eu/our_labs/eurl-ecvam

European Society for Alternatives to Animal Testing (EUSAAT)
www.eusaat.org

Humane Research Australia
www.humaneresearch.org.au

Interagency Coordinating Committee on the Validation of Alternative Methods (ICCVAM)
http://iccvam.niehs.nih.gov

InVitro International
www.invitrointl.com/about/index.htm

Johns Hopkins Center for Alternatives to Animal Testing (CAAT)
http://caat.jhsph.edu

World Congress on Alternatives and Animal Use in the Life Sciences
www.wc8.ccac.ca

General Veganism

American Vegan Society
www.americanvegan.org

Cowspiracy (Film)
www.cowspiracy.com

Earthlings (Film)
www.earthlings.com

Forks Over Knives (Film)
www.forksoverknives.com/the-film/

Malzoism.org
www.malzoism.org

Vegan Outreach
www.veganoutreach.org

Vegan Society
www.vegansociety.com

Vegan Starter Kit
www.vegankit.com

Further Reading

Aysha Akhtar, *Animals and Public Health,* Palgrave Macmillan, 2012.

Bailey, J., "Monkey-based Research on Human Disease: The Implications of Genetic Differences," *Alternatives to Laboratory Animals (ATLA)* 42, no. 5 (2014).

Bailey, J., Capaldo, T., Conlee, K., & Thew, M., "Nonhuman Primates Mean Less, Not More, Human Medical Progress," *Nature Medicine,* no.14 (10) (2008): 1011–12.

Bailey, J., "How Well Do Animal Teratology Studies Predict Human Hazard?" *Biogenic Amines* 19 no.2 (2005): 97–145.

Bailey, J., "NHP Genetic Similarities Offer No Results" Response to Morgan et al. "The Use of Nonhuman Primate Models in HIV Vaccine Development," *PLoS Medicine* 5 no.8 (2008): 173.

Bailey, J., Balcombe, J. & Capaldo, T., *Chimpanzee Research: An Examination of Its Contribution to Biomedical Knowledge and Efficacy in Combating Human Diseases, and Supplement,* Project R&R (2007).

Balcombe JP, Barnard ND, Sandusky C., "Laboratory routines cause animal stress," *Contemporary Topics* 43 (2004): 42–51.

Bross I., "How animal research can kill you," *The AV Magazine,* November 1983.

Capaldo, T., "The Psychological Effects of Using Animals," *Alternatives to Laboratory Animals* 32 (Supp.1) (2004): 525–31.

Covino Jr., Joseph., *Lab Animal Abuse: Vivisection Exposed!*. New Humanity Press, 1990.

Davis, K., "The Experimental Use of Chickens and Other Birds in Biomedical and Agricultural Research," *United Poultry Concerns* (2003).

Garber K., "Realistic rodents? Debate grows over new mouse models of cancer," *J Natl Cancer Inst.* 98 (2006): 1176–8.

Goodman J., *et al.*, "Trends in Animal Use at US Research Facilities," *Journal of Medical Ethics* 0(2015): 1–3.

Groff, K., Bachli, E., Lansdowne, M., and Capaldo, T., "Review of Evidence of Environmental Impacts of Animal Research and Testing," *Environments*, (2014).

Hackam D., Redelmeier D., "Translation of Research Evidence From Animals to Human," The Journal of the American Medical Association 296 (2006): 1731–2.

Langley G, Evans T, Holgate ST, Jones A., "Replacing animal experiments: choices, chances, and challenges," *BioEssays* 29 (2007): 918–26.

Lee M-Y, Park CB, Dordick JS, Clark DS., "Metabolizing enzyme toxicology assay chip (MetaChip) for high-throughput microscale toxicity analysis," *Proc Natl Acad Sci.* 102 (2005): 983–7.

Lee M-Y, Kumar RA, Sukumaran SM, Hogg MG, Clark DS, Dordick JS., "Three-dimensional cellular microarray for high-throughput toxicology assays," *Proc Natl Acad Sci.* 105 (2008): 59–63.

Mukerjee M., "Speaking for the Animals: A Veterinarian Analyzes the Turf Battles That Have Transformed the Animal Laboratory," Scientific American, Aug. 2004.

Perel P, Roberts I, Sena E, et al., "Comparison of treatment effects between animal experiments and clinical trials: systematic review," *BMJ* 334 (2006): 197.

Pound P., Ebrahim S., Sandercock P., Bracken MB, Roberts I., "Where is the evidence that animal research benefits humans?" *BMJ* 328 (2004): 514–7.

Pound P. Bracken M., "Is Animal Research Sufficiently Evidence Based To Be A Cornerstone of Biomedical Research?" *BMJ* (2014): 348.

Robinson M.K., et al., "Validity and Ethics of the Human 4-h Patch Test as an Alternative Method to Assess Acute Skin Irritation Potential," Contact Dermatitis, 45 (2001): 1–12.

Seok J., et al., "Genomic Responses in Mouse Models Poorly Mimic Human Inflammatory Diseases," Proceedings of the National Academy of Sciences 110 (2013): 3507–12.

Shaw, George Bernard, *Shaw on Vivisection*, Alethea Publications, 1951.

Watts G., "Alternatives to animal experimentation," *BMJ* 334 (2007): 182–4.

ABOUT THE AUTHOR

Michael Slusher worked as a research biologist for many years before pursuing a career that was more in line with his ethics and morals. Still interested in animals, he earned a degree in Anthropology, with a focus on Zooarchaelogy—the study of animal remains as found within a human archaeological context. After recognizing the cruel and exploitative role humans play in the lives of animals, he became dedicated to vegan education and outreach. This book is his first major step towards that goal, and ultimately, he hopes to run an animal rescue that focuses on sanctuary for former laboratory animals. He and his wife currently reside in the Eastern United States and are owned by many rescued cats.